Student Study Guide

to accompany

The Inclusive Classroom
Strategies for Effective Instruction

Second Edition

Margo A. Mastropieri and Thomas E. Scruggs
George Mason University

Prepared by
Janna Siegel Robertson
University of Memphis

Upper Saddle River, New Jersey
Columbus, Ohio

Vice President and Executive Publisher: Jeffery W. Johnston
AcquisitionsEditor: Allyson P. Sharp
Development Editor: Heather Doyle Fraser
Editorial Assistant: Kathleen S. Burk
Production Editor: Sheryl Glicker Langner
Design Coordinator: Diane C. Lorenzo
Cover Designer: Ali Mohrman
Cover art: © Nicky Williams, a participating artist of VSA arts, *http://www.vsarts.org/*
Production Manager: Laura Messerly
Director of Marketing: Ann Castel Davis
Marketing Manager: Amy June
Marketing Coordinator: Tyra Poole

Pearson Prentice Hall™ is a trademark of Pearson Education, Inc.
Pearson® is a registered trademark of Pearson plc
Prentice Hall® is a registered trademark of Pearson Education, Inc.
Merrill® is a registered trademark of Pearson Education, Inc.

Pearson Education Ltd.
Pearson Education Singapore Pte. Ltd.
Pearson Education Canada, Ltd.
Pearson Education—Japan

Pearson Education Australia Pty. Limited
Pearson Education North Asia Ltd.
Pearson Educación de Mexico, S.A. de C.V.
Pearson Education Malaysia Pte. Ltd.

10 9 8 7 6 5 4 3 2 1
ISBN: 0-13-114373-5

Table of Contents

Chapter 1: Introduction to Inclusive Teaching   1

Chapter 2: Collaboration: Partnerships and Procedures   7

Chapter 3: Teaching Students with Higher-Incidence Disabilities   13

Chapter 4: Teaching Students with Lower-Incidence Disabilities   19

Chapter 5: Teaching Students with Other Special Learning Needs   25

Chapter 6: Effective Instruction for All Students   31

Chapter 7: Improving Classroom Behavior and Social Skills   37

Chapter 8: Promoting Inclusion with Classroom Peers   43

Chapter 9: Enhancing Motivation and Affect   49

Chapter 10: Improving Attention and Memory   55

Chapter 11: Teaching Study Skills   61

Chapter 12: Assessment   67

Chapter 13: Literacy   73

Chapter 14: Mathematics   79

Chapter 15: Science and Social Studies   87

Chapter 16: Art, Music, Physical Education, Foreign Languages, Vocational Education, and Transitions   93

Answer Key   99

Chapter 1: Introduction to Inclusive Teaching

Objectives

After studying this chapter, you should be able to:

- Understand federal laws protecting the educational services for students with disabilities.
- Compare and contrast the issues surrounding inclusive instruction for students with disabilities.
- Analyze several important court cases relating to students with disabilities, presenting a progression of increasing rights for students with disabilities.
- Describe the continuum of services available to students with special needs and the "least-restrictive environment" concept.
- Identify the disability categories served under IDEA.
- Summarize and describe the legal foundations, litigation, and legislation of students with disabilities, such as IDEA (Individuals with Disabilities Education Act), Section 504 (Vocational Rehabilitation Act), and ADA (Americans with Disabilities Act).

Chapter Outline

I. WHAT ARE THE EDUCATIONAL RIGHTS FOR INDIVIDUALS WITH DISABILITIES?
II. THE LEAST-RESTRICTIVE ENVIRONMENT
    A. Where Are the Students with Disabilities Served?
    B. Mainstreaming and Inclusion
    C. Who Is Served Under IDEA?
    D. Other Instances of Classroom Divers
III. LEGAL FOUNDATIONS
    A. Legal Proceedings and Legislation
    B. Section 504
    C. Americans with Disabilities Act
    D. Individuals with Disabilities Education Act (IDEA)
    E. No Child Left Behind Act of 2001
IV. MODELS OF SERVICE DELIVERY
    A. The Continuum of Services
    B. Where Are Most Students with Disabilities Served?
    C. What Are General Education Classroom and Consultation Services?
    D. What Are Resource and Self-Contained Services?
    E. Special Schools and Special Facilities.
    F. What Other Related Services Are Available?
    G. Inclusion Movements
        1. Regular Education Initiative
        2. Full Inclusion Movement
    H. What Does This Debate Mean for Teachers?
    I. Teacher Attitudes
        1. Volunteerism
        2. Mandated Inclusion
        3. How do these situations compare?
V. SUMMARY

- In 1975, Public Law 94-142 (IDEA) was passed. This law, and its subsequent amendments, established the rights of students with disabilities to a free, appropriate public education. It further provided that this education would take place, to the maximum extent possible, in the least restrictive environment. Prior to the passage of this law, students with special needs were routinely excluded from public school.
- IDEA provides for special services for disability areas including autism, hearing impairments, mental retardation, multiple disabilities, orthopedic impairments, other health impairments, serious emotional disturbance, specific learning disabilities, speech or language impairments, traumatic brain injury, visual impairments, and deaf-blindness. However, other groups of students may also require special adaptations by general education teachers, including students who are culturally or linguistically diverse, students at risk for school failure, and students with gifts or talents.
- Other court rulings and federal laws, such as Section 504 and the Americans with Disabilities Act, have provided for nondiscriminatory treatment of individuals with disabilities.
- Six important principles in IDEA are (1) zero reject, (2) nondiscriminatory testing, (3) appropriate education, (4) least restrictive environment, (5) due process, and (6) parent participation.
- Current educational practice provides for a continuum of services for students with disabilities, from full-time placement in the regular education classroom, to special residential schools. Most students with disabilities today are served in regular education classrooms.
- Some controversy today exists over the concept of "full inclusion," the full-time placement of students with disabilities in regular classrooms. Concerned individuals on both sides of this issue have raised important points.
- Most teachers favor some form of inclusion for their own classes. However, teachers report a need for sufficient time, training, and resources in order to teach effectively in inclusive classrooms. When these supports are provided, attitudes toward inclusive teaching also improve.

Multiple Choice

Select the statement that best answers each multiple choice question.

1. Which is NOT one of the disability categories included and served under Individuals with Disabilities Education Act (IDEA)?

    a. Communication disorders
    b. Students at risk for school failure
    c. Hearing impairments
    d. Orthopedic impairments

2. Which of the following is one of the principles of The Individuals with Disabilities Education Act (IDEA)?

    a. For students with disabilities to receive the best possible educational services
    b. For students with disabilities to receive a free and appropriate education
    c. To educate students with disabilities in the general education setting
    d. To encourage every student to graduate high school regardless of ability

3. What term means, "students with disabilities must be educated in a setting least removed from the general education classroom?"

    a. Full inclusion
    b. Mainstreaming
    c. Least-Restrictive Environment
    d. Resource Room

4. Which of the following educational placements represent an example from the "Continuum of Services"?

    a. Vocational placement in an area school district
    b. School suspension, either at the school or at home
    c. General education classroom with resource room services
    d. Tutoring, including peer and cross-age

5. Which of the following is NOT a related service provided under IDEA to assist students with disabilities?

    a. Parent Counseling
    b. Reduced insurance/medical rates
    c. Physical/Occupational Therapy
    d. Special transportation

6. In a _____ model of instruction, students with specialized needs receive all or most of their major instruction from special education teachers.

    a. self-contained
    b. full inclusion
    c. mainstreaming
    d. least-restrictive environment

7. In the 1980s, what movement was initiated to provide a model for educating students with disabilities—particularly those students with mild and moderate disabilities—totally within the general education environment?

    a. The Full Inclusion Movement
    b. Regular Education Initiative
    c. Least-Restrictive Environment Movement
    d. The Special Education Movement

8. Which of the following benefits is NOT usually predicted for the full-inclusion model?

    a. Reduces stigma
    b. More efficient
    c. Promotes equality
    d. Professional Development

True or False

Determine if each statement is true or false.

1. The Individuals with Disabilities Education Act (IDEA) is a federal law stating ALL students are entitled to a "free and appropriate education."

    a. TRUE
    b. FALSE

2. Today, nearly seventy-five percent of students with disabilities are served primarily in general education classrooms.

    a. TRUE
    b. FALSE

3. Section 504 (of the Vocational Rehabilitation Act) is a law preventing discrimination of students with disabilities in all federally funded institutions and workplaces.

    a. TRUE
    b. FALSE

4. Least Restrictive Environment means to teach students with disabilities in the general education classroom.

    a. TRUE
    b. FALSE

5. The individualized family service plan (IFSP) replaces the individualized education plan (IEP) when other family members also need special services.

    a. TRUE
    b. FALSE

6. Many proponents of full inclusion believe that full-time placement in the general education classroom is a basic right of all students, including students with disabilities.

    a. TRUE
    b. FALSE

7. Teachers are given the choice of whether or not to include students with disabilities in their classes.

    a. TRUE
    b. FALSE

Short Answer/Essay

1. What are the major differences between historical and current practices toward individuals with disabilities?

2. How do the 6 principles of IDEA protect the rights of students and parents? Give an example for each principle.

3. Give examples of how a student with disabilities may be stigmatized by (1) pulling him or her out of the classroom to receive special education services and (2) providing him or her special education services in the general education classroom.

4. What does the expression "special education is a service, not a place" mean when discussing the continuum of services?

5. What laws or portions of a law are the following scenarios violating?
   - Jose is tested for special education after his Non-English speaking parents initial a consent form in English.

   - Jamal is given an IQ in English even though he speaks only Arabic.

- Julie is told she cannot work as a paraprofessional since she has mild cerebral palsy and uses a walker.

- Jacqueline, who has muscular dystrophy, is told that she cannot attend her neighborhood school since they do not have accessibility ramps for her wheelchair.

- The school district changed the number of hours Jeremy is receiving special education services and then informed the parents without holding an IEP meeting.

For more activities related to chapter content, go to the Activities module in chapter 1 of the Companion Website at www.prenhall.com/mastropieri.

Chapter 2: Collaboration: Partnerships and Procedures

Objectives

After studying this chapter, you should be able to:

- List and describe the six major steps involved in effective communication to establish collaboration.
- Describe the general education prereferral process, such as establishing timelines, intervention strategies, and consultations.
- Identify the educational evaluation or assessment steps as well as the key components comprising the case conference committee and IEP program.
- Gain understanding of the importance of partnerships between special and general educators.
- Identify the benefits and potential barriers to co-teaching and research supporting the collaboration among educators.
- Understand the roles and responsibilities, background, and importance of communicating with paraprofessionals.
- Describe the importance of positive communication and collaboration with parents and families.

Chapter Outline

I. COLLABORATION TO ESTABLISH NEED
   A.   Shared Goals
II. EFFECTIVE COMMUNICATION
       1.   Active listening
       2.   Depersonalize situations
       3.   Find common goals
       4.   Brainstorm possible solutions
       5.   Summarize goals and solutions
       6.   Follow up to monitor progress
III. COLLABORATION AND COMMUNICATION FOR INTERVENTION
       1.   General education prereferral request
   B.   The Intervention Process
       1.   Establishing timelines
       2.   Intervention strategies
       3.   Prereferral consultations
IV. COLLABORATION FOR REFERRALS AND PLACEMENTS
       1.   The educational evaluation or assessment step
       2.   The case conference committee
       3.   Ease the concern of parents and students
       4.   Related services
       5.   The Individualized Education Program (IEP)
       6.   Writing goals and objectives
       7.   Transition services
       8.   Monitoring IEPs
           a.   Due process
           b.   Annual reviews
V. COLLABORATION AS PARTNERSHIPS
   A.   Partnerships Between Special and General Educators

    B.   Designing Adaptations
    C.   Co-Teaching
        1.   Research support
    D.   Collaboration with Paraprofessionals
        1.   Background of paraprofessionals
        2.   Roles and responsibilities of paraprofessionals
        3.   Communicating with paraprofessionals
    E.   Parents and Families as Partners
        1.   Variability in backgrounds and family structures
        2.   Positive communication
        3.   Communicating about homework
        4.   Parent advisory groups
        5.   Handling disability issues
        6.   Disability resources
        7.   Disagreements
VI.   SUMMARY

Chapter Overview

- Collaboration—involving cooperation, effective communication, shared problem-solving, planning, and finding solutions—is the process for ensuring that all students receive the free, appropriate public education mandated by IDEA.
- Both schools and parents have responsibilities under IDEA. Partnerships can involve parents and professionals representing a variety of areas, including general and special education teachers, administrators, school psychologists, counselors, social workers, and community mental health agencies.
- Effective communication is critical for successful collaboration. Effective communication involves active listening, depersonalizing situations, finding common goals, brainstorming steps for achieving common goals, identifying possible solutions, and summarizing the conversation. Following these steps can be very important in solving problems.
- General education prereferral interventions are steps taken by schools to promote success in the regular classroom, before deciding on referral for special education. These actions can involve general and special education teachers, specialists, administrators, parents, and students.
- Effective communication and collaboration is particularly important in the referral and placement process. For case conference committees to perform successfully, effective communication is essential.
- Building effective collaborative partnerships is one of the most significant tasks of a successful inclusive teacher. With effective teamwork, solutions can be found to any number of problems.
- Collaboration can take the form of consultation, in which special education teachers work together to decide upon intervention strategies for a specific student. Communication can take the form of notes, informal conversations, or scheduled meetings.
- Collaboration can also take the form of co-teaching, in which a general education and special education teacher teach together in an inclusive classroom setting. These models are (1) one teacher and one assistant, (2) station teaching, (3) parallel teaching, (4) alternative teaching, and (5) team teaching. Teachers should consider all models, and keep records of their own collaboration, to determine which best fits the needs of the students.
- Teachers must also collaborate effectively with paraprofessionals, in order to maximize the success of the inclusive classroom. Teachers should carefully consider the background of the paraprofessional, outline roles and responsibilities, and communicate effectively at all times.

- Effective collaboration with parents is a key to effective inclusive teaching. Teachers should consider variability in family backgrounds and family structures, and maintain close, positive contacts with parents throughout the year.

Multiple Choice

Select the statement that best answers each multiple choice question.

1. Which is NOT a component of effective communication?

    a. Active listening
    b. Follow up to monitor progress
    c. Identifying common goals
    d. Constructive criticism

2. Information often submitted with a formal prereferral intervention request includes:

    a. Documentation of observations
    b. Student work samples
    c. Disciplinary actions
    d. All of the above

3. Changing seating positions and rearranging desks are types of

    a. environmental modifications.
    b. classroom management modifications.
    c. adjustments in classroom atmosphere.
    d. modifications in classroom routines.

4. Which of the following is generally considered to be the most effective co-teaching model?

    a. Station teaching
    b. Parallel teaching
    c. Alternative teaching
    d. None of the above

5. Services identified by the case conference committee as related services include:

    a. Physical or occupational therapy
    b. Parent counseling
    c. Medical services
    d. All of the above

6. Individualized Transition Plans (ITPs) are required to be written into student IEPs beginning at _____ years of age.

    a. 5
    b. 8
    c. 14
    d. 17

7. Short-term objectives included on an IEP do NOT include which of the following?

    a. Meeting the disability needs to enable participation in the general education curriculum
    b. Meeting educational needs resulting from the disability
    c. Meeting annual goals
    d. All of the above are included as short-term objectives

8. Re-evaluations of students with IEPs can be requested:

    a. Annually
    b. Bi-annually
    c. At any time
    d. Re-evaluations are not needed because evaluations are done annually

9. Due process refers to

    a. the prereferral process.
    b. the IEP process.
    c. how conflicts between parents and schools are resolved.
    d. how a student's vocational or employment training needs will be addressed.

10. A _____ assists in mediating disputes and/or conflicts between parents and the school district regarding the student's education or disagreements on eligibility, outcomes of the educational evaluation, or other aspects of the IEP.

    a. mediator
    b. building principal
    c. due process
    d. school counselor

True or False

Determine if each statement is true or false.

1. The prereferral intervention process is a part of the special education IEP process.

    a. TRUE
    b. FALSE

2. An individualized education program includes a statement explaining the extent to which a student may not be participating with children without disabilities.

   a. TRUE
   b. FALSE

3. Transportation services are NOT relevant to a student's IEP.

   a. TRUE
   b. FALSE

4. In the co-teaching strategy "alternative teaching," teachers teach similar content but may use different approaches depending on student needs.

   a. TRUE
   b. FALSE

5. Mediation is a voluntary process that must be requested by both parties.

   a. TRUE
   b. FALSE

6. Parents are clear on their roles in inclusive collaboration.

   a. TRUE
   b. FALSE

7. Paraprofessionals are only responsible for non-educational tasks.

   a. TRUE
   b. FALSE

Short Answer/Essay

1. What are the steps to effective communication? Give an example of a time you had to work on a project with others and went through each of the processes to collaboratively accomplish the task?

2. Which of the following IEP objectives would be easier for you to follow as a teacher?

   A. Johan will learn multiplication this year on grade level.
   B. When given a teacher made test of 30 multiplication problems with single digits on a timed test, Johan will complete 25 out of 30 problems correctly in 5 minutes.

What would you do if you did not understand an IEP objective for one of your students?

3. You are told to co-teach with a special education teacher. You have always taught every subject to your elementary students and are a bit reluctant to let someone else take over your class. But you always felt you could do much more with another adult in the classroom. What co-teaching arrangement would you prefer? Is there a subject area you would be willing to give up? Or would you only be comfortable with him or her working in a supportive role? What benefits would there be if one of you were teaching while the other was monitoring students' understanding and comprehension?

For more activities related to chapter content, go to the Activities module in chapter 2 of the Companion Website at www.prenhall.com/mastropieri.

Chapter 3: Teaching Students with Higher-Incidence Disabilities

Objectives

After studying this chapter, you should be able to:

- Describe and discuss the prevalence and characteristics of students with speech or language impairments.
- Describe and discuss the prevalence and characteristics of students with learning disabilities.
- Describe and discuss the prevalence and characteristics of students with mental retardation.
- Describe and discuss the prevalence and characteristics of students with emotional disturbance.
- List, describe, and be able to recommend adaptations and modifications to promote inclusion of students with higher-incidence disabilities.

Chapter Outline

I.   SPEECH OR LANGUAGE IMPAIRMENTS
   A.   Prevalence, Definitions, and Characteristics
      1.   Examples and characteristics of speech disorders
      2.   Examples and characteristics of language disorders
   B.   Causes of Speech or Language Impairments
   C.   Issues in Identification and Assessment of Speech or Language Impairments
   D.   Classroom Adaptations for Students with Speech or Language Impairments
      1.   Adapt the physical environment
      2.   Adapt materials
      3.   Adapt instruction
      4.   Adapt evaluation

II.   LEARNING DISABILITIES
   A.   Prevalence and Definitions of Learning Disabilities
   B.   Causes of Learning Disabilities
   C.   Issues in Identification and Assessment of Learning Disabilities
      1.   Specificity
      2.   Discrepancy
   D.   Characteristics of Learning Disabilities
      1.   Language and literacy
      2.   Mathematics
      3.   Attention and memory
      4.   Thinking and reasoning
      5.   Metacognitive abilities, including study skills, learning strategies, and organizational strategies
      6.   Social-emotional functioning
      7.   Generalization and application
   E.   Classroom Adaptations for Students with Learning Disabilities

III.   MENTAL RETARDATION
   A.   Prevalence and Definitions of Mental Retardation
   B.   Causes of Mental Retardation
      1.   Genetic factors
      2.   Brain factors

           3.   Environmental influences
    C.   Issues in Identification and Assessment of Mental Retardation
    D.   Characteristics of Mental Retardation
           1.   Intellectual and cognitive functioning
           2.   Social and adaptive behavior
           3.   Language
           4.   Academic skills
    E.   Classroom Adaptations for Students with Mental Retardation
           1.   Preparations
           2.   Monitor peer relationships
           3.   Instructional modifications
IV.   EMOTIONAL DISTURBANCE
    A.   Prevalence and Definitions
    B.   Causes of Emotional Disturbance
    C.   Issues in Identification and Assessment of Emotional Disturbance
    D.   Characteristics of Emotional Disturbance
           1.   Social behavior
           2.   Affective characteristics
           3.   Academic characteristics
    E.   Classroom Adaptations for Students with Emotional Disturbance
           1.   Preparing the class
           2.   Teaching adaptations
           3.   Other adaptations
V.   SUMMARY

Chapter Overview

- Approximately 90% of the population of students with disabilities have learning disabilities, mental retardation, emotional disturbance, or speech or language impairments. Most students with higher-incidence disabilities are served in the general education classroom.
- In many cases, causes of these high-incidence disabilities are unknown, although a variety of biological and environmental explanations have been proposed. Speech disorders may exist as voice, articulation, or fluency disorders; language disorders may involve difficulties with phonology, morphology, syntax, semantics, or pragmatics of language use.
- Students with learning disabilities comprise about half of students with higher-incidence disabilities. These students may exhibit specific problems in basic skill areas, as well as areas such as language, attention, memory, and metacognition.
- Students with mental retardation exhibit deficiencies in intellectual functioning, and corresponding levels of adaptive behavior. These students also may exhibit learning problems related to language, social behavior, attention, reasoning, and problem solving.
- Students with emotional disturbance may exhibit problems in classroom behavior, social relations, or may exhibit disorders of affect, such as anxiety or depression.
- A variety of adaptations in the physical environment, instructional materials, instructional procedures, and evaluation procedures can make the general education classroom a positive learning experience for students with higher-incidence disabilities.

Multiple Choice

Select the statement that best answers each multiple choice question.

1. Higher-incidence disability areas comprise approximately _____ of students served under IDEA.

    a. 10%
    b. 25%
    c. 50%
    d. 90%

2. Classroom adaptations for students with speech or language impairments include:

    a. Providing an open and accepting classroom
    b. Using technology such as audiotapes
    c. Alternative or augmentative communication techniques
    d. All of the above

3. Lisping is an example of a(n)

    a. voice disorder.
    b. articulation disorder.
    c. fluency disorder.
    d. language disorder.

4. The disability area most widely represented in general education classes is

    a. communication disorders.
    b. serious emotional disturbance.
    c. learning disabilities.
    d. mental retardation.

5. Which condition does the federal definition of learning disabilities NOT include?

    a. Brain injury
    b. Dyslexia
    c. Minimal brain dysfunction
    d. Mental retardation

6. Students with moderate mental retardation represent a range of functioning represented by IQ scores between about:

    a. 35 to 54.
    b. 45 to 65.
    c. 55 to 70.
    d. Below 20.

7. _____ is an example of a genetic disorder also referred to as Trisomy 21.

    a. Asperger's syndrome
    b. Tourette syndrome
    c. Acquired Prader-Willi syndrome
    d. Down syndrome

8. Which statement is true of students with emotional disturbance?

    a. Boys outnumber girls 5 to 1
    b. Both boys and girls are equally represented
    c. Girls outnumber boys 5 to 1
    d. Girls are not considered to have emotional disturbance

9. Which is a criterion under IDEA (1996) regarding emotional disturbance?

    a. Inability to exhibit appropriate behavior
    b. Inappropriate affect such as depression
    c. Inappropriate manifestation of physical symptoms or fears
    d. All of the above

10. Which of the following disorders are associated with emotional disturbance ?

    a. Selective mutism
    b. Mental retardation
    c. Aphasia
    d. All of the above

True or False

Determine if each statement is true or false.

1. Stuttering is a common articulation disorder.

    a. TRUE
    b. FALSE

2. Semantics refers to the meanings of words used in language.

    a. TRUE
    b. FALSE

3. While most students with learning disabilities have difficulty learning to read, students with learning disabilities rarely exhibit difficulties learning mathematics.

    a. TRUE
    b. FALSE

4. Children with learning disabilities are usually not identified until they enter school.

    a. TRUE
    b. FALSE

5. Fewer than half (about 45%) of students with mental retardation have mild or moderate disabilities.

    a. TRUE
    b. FALSE

6. Social maladjustment such as juvenile delinquency is a component of the IDEA definition of emotional disturbance.

    a. TRUE
    b. FALSE

7. Students with emotional disturbance may not exhibit aggressive behaviors.

    a. TRUE
    b. FALSE

Short Answer/Essay

1. Jacqui is very shy and will not speak in public. She has a speech impairment (lisp) that makes her self-conscious in your 3rd grade class. She does have a few close friends she will whisper to, and she will also speak to you if no one is around. You have oral book reports due next week in class. You want to encourage Jacqui to speak since she is supposed to practice her speech therapy, but you do not want to put her in a stressful situation.

    a. What are the strengths and needs of the student?
    b. What are 3 possible modifications or interventions you could use to help Jacqui to be successful on her oral report?

2. There will usually be students with high-incidence disabilities in your classroom every year. Research studies have demonstrated that adaptation used for students with special needs work even better for students without disabilities. Choose 3 suggestions from this chapter that you believe will help all of your students to achieve.

3. Many students have organizational problems (so do many teachers!). What are some ways that you can organize your classroom at the beginning of the year to assist your students and yourself in organization?

4. If a 14-year-old student with mental retardation wanted to sit on your lap and hug you, would you think that action was appropriate? Why or why not? What would you say to the student?

For more activities related to chapter content, go to the Activities module in chapter 3 of the Companion Website at www.prenhall.com/mastropieri.

Chapter 4: Teaching Students with Lower-Incidence Disabilities

Objectives

After studying this chapter, you should be able to:

- Describe and discuss the prevalence and characteristics of students with visual impairments.
- Describe and discuss the prevalence and characteristics of students with hearing impairments.
- Describe and discuss the prevalence and characteristics of students with physical disabilities and other health impairments.
- Describe and discuss the prevalence and characteristics of students with severe and multiple disabilities.
- Describe and discuss the prevalence and characteristics of students with autism.
- List, describe, and be able to recommend adaptations and modifications to promote inclusion of students with lower-incidence disabilities.

Chapter Outline

I. VISUAL IMPAIRMENTS
   A. Prevalence, Definitions, and Characteristics
   B. Classroom Adaptations for Students with Visual Impairments
II. HEARING IMPAIRMENTS
   A. Prevalence, Definitions, and Characteristics
   B. Educational Programming
   C. Classroom Adaptations for Students with Hearing Impairments
      1. Adapt evaluation
III. PHYSICAL DISABILITIES AND OTHER HEALTH IMPAIRMENTS
   A. Prevalence, Definitions, and Characteristics
   B. Physical and Health-Related Disabilities
      1. Cerebral palsy
      2. Spina bifida
      3. Muscular dystrophy
      4. Traumatic brain injury
      5. Epilepsy
      6. Arthritis
      7. Asthma and allergies
      8. Diabetes
      9. Fetal alcohol syndrome and other disorders
      10. Acquired Immune Deficiency Syndrome (AIDS)
   C. Classroom Adaptations for Students with Physical Disabilities and Other Health Impairments
      1. Medical guidelines
         a. Be aware of medications
         b. Plan for fatigue
         c. Establish emergency procedures
         d. Plan for seizures
         e. Moving and positioning students
         f. Adapt for chronic medical conditions

g.   Dealing with terminal illness
2.   Prepare the class
3.   Adapt the physical environment
4.   Adapt instructional materials
5.   Adapt instruction
6.   Adapt evaluation

IV.   SEVERE AND MULTIPLE DISABILITIES
  A.   Prevalence, Definitions, and Characteristics
     1.   Educational placement considerations
  B.   Classroom Adaptations for Students with Severe Disabilities
     1.   Establish good working relationships with paraprofessionals
     2.   Increase disability awareness
     3.   Conceptualize inclusive instruction
     4.   Adapt instructional delivery systems
     5.   Consider special health-care needs
     6.   Classroom adaptations

V.   AUTISM
  A.   Prevalence, Definitions, and Characteristics
  B.   Classroom Adaptations for Students with Autism
     1.   Establish effective communication
        a.   Facilitated communication
     2.   Develop social competence

VI.   SUMMARY

Chapter Overview

- Lower-incidence disabilities occur less frequently in the general population than other disabilities areas. Lower-incidence disabilities include visual impairments, hearing impairments, physical disabilities, other health impairments, severe and multiple disabilities, and autism.
- Individuals with visual impairments represent the smallest categories of exceptionality. Students may have very low vision to no vision. These students may have difficulty learning unless adaptations are made, such as arranging the physical environment for easy accessibility, enhancing printed materials, using Braille and oral formats, and using concrete tactile and three-dimensional examples.
- Students with hearing impairments have mild to severe hearing losses. Individuals with mild to moderate hearing impairments usually wear hearing aids, while individuals who are deaf use sign language, total communication or some aural techniques for communication. Students may require specific language, communication, and social skills instruction.
- Students with physical disabilities may exhibit difficulties using their arms, legs, or both arms and legs. Some of these students may exhibit problems with communication. Specific adaptations for increasing mobility, assisting with fine motor control, and improving communication skills help students become more independent and successful.
- Students with other health impairments may have serious medical needs that require special attention and that restrict their learning in school. Coordination with medical professionals while monitoring health and educational needs helps these students with school success.
- Students with severe disabilities have severe mental retardation and exhibit difficulties in cognition, adaptive behavior, academic, social, self-help, problem-solving, attention, and memory areas.

- Students with autism may have mild to severe difficulties, but usually have serious difficulties with social behavior. Students with more severe autism have difficulties with language, communication, cognitive, attention, memory, and basic skills.
- Arrange special classroom procedures for emergency situations for classrooms containing individuals with lower-incidence disabilities. These individuals may miss the usual safety alert systems, tire more easily, or have special medical or mobility needs that require special preparation.
- A variety of adaptations in the physical environment, instructional materials, and evaluation procedures makes the general education classroom a positive learning experience for students with lower-incidence disabilities.

Multiple Choice

Select the statement that best answers each multiple choice question.

1. Individuals with _____ comprise one of the smallest disability areas, accounting for only about 0.5% of individuals with disabilities classified under IDEA.

   a. hearing impairments
   b. visual impairments
   c. physical and other health impairments
   d. severe and multiple disabilities

2. Potential causes of hearing impairments include:

   a. Maternal rubella
   b. Diabetic retinopathy
   c. Nephritis
   d. All of the above

3. Orthopedic impairments involve damage to the:

   a. Nervous system
   b. Skeletal system
   c. Circulatory system
   d. All of the above

4. Health conditions referred to as Other Health Impairments include:

   a. Asperger's syndrome
   b. Maternal rubella
   c. Allergies and asthma
   d. All of the above

5. _____ is a common neurological disorder that causes permanent disorders of movement and positions.

   a. Cerebral palsy
   b. Spina bifida
   c. Muscular dystrophy
   d. Epilepsy

6. Commonly provided adaptations for students with traumatic brain injuries include:

    a. Dimming light levels in the classroom
    b. Providing a shortened school day
    c. Dietary modifications
    d. All of the above

7. Which of the following is true of muscular dystrophy?

    a. It is a contagious disease.
    b. All forms are life threatening.
    c. Motor difficulties are apparent at birth.
    d. Children should be lifted only by those with explicit training.

8. _____ is an inherited condition in which sugar is not metabolized correctly due to insufficient production of insulin in the pancreas.

    a. Tay-Sach's disease
    b. Asperger's syndrome
    c. William's syndrome
    d. Diabetes

9. It is estimated that _____ of individuals with autism may never develop language.

    a. 10%
    b. 25%
    c. 50%
    d. 75%

10. A common characteristic of autism is:

    a. Orthopedic impairments
    b. Stereotypic behavior
    c. Early language development
    d. All of the above

True or False

Determine if each statement is true or false.

1. Individuals are classified as legally blind if their visual acuity is less than 20/100 with corrective lenses.

    a. TRUE
    b. FALSE

2. Retinitis pigmentosa is a common cause of hearing impairment.

    a. TRUE
    b. FALSE

3. Cerebral palsy is progressive in nature, which means it worsens over time.

    a. TRUE
    b. FALSE

4. In any seizure, do not place any object between the teeth of the affected person.

    a. TRUE
    b. FALSE

5. Children will chronic illnesses should do most of their work in the afternoon after they have had a chance to warm-up in the morning.

    a. TRUE
    b. FALSE

6. "Curriculum overlapping" is a technique for including students with severe and multiple disabilities into general education class curriculum and activities.

    a. TRUE
    b. FALSE

7. Teachers should not ask about medications that a child might be taking since that violates the patient-doctor confidentiality.

    a. TRUE
    b. FALSE

Short Answer/Essay

1. Jill has diabetes and has to watch her sugar intake. She participates in all of your elementary class activities with no problems. But you like to reward the students with candy at times. Plus there are several parties planned for the year. You don't want to exclude Jill from the sweets but you do not think it is fair to deprive your whole class either. You also want to make sure she is not eating something she should not. What can you do to make sure Jill is included but not singled out in front of the class?

2. Teachers who are new to teaching students with low-incidence disabilities may not know how to handle interactions with students with special needs. What would you do in the following situations?

- A student limps by your classroom on her way to lunch. You notice her since it is your planning time. She wears crutches since she has cerebral palsy. She also makes soft whimpering sounds when she passes by and looks at you with sad eyes. Since she does not weigh much you want to carry her to the cafeteria. What should you do or say? Why?
- You see some observers walking by a male high school student in a wheelchair who is in an aisle. As the women observers walk by, the student pats them on their posteriors. So far no one has said anything to the student. You are the next one who needs to walk by him. What should you do or say? Why?

3. Classroom arrangement can be very important for students with certain types of disabilities. What are some classroom accommodations you would make for a student with a wheelchair? What are some classroom accommodations you would make for a student who is blind and uses a cane?

4. What plan of action would you have if a student has a seizure? How would you be able to take care of your class and the student?

For more activities related to chapter content, go to the Activities module in chapter 4 of the Companion Website at www.prenhall.com/mastropieri.

Chapter 5: Teaching Students with Other Special Learning Needs

Objectives

After studying this chapter, you should be able to:

- Describe and discuss the prevalence and characteristics of students with Attention Deficit Disorder (ADD) and Attention Deficit Hyperactivity Disorder (ADHD).
- Describe and discuss the prevalence and characteristics of students who are gifted, creative, or talented.
- Describe and discuss the prevalence and characteristics of students from culturally and linguistically diverse backgrounds.
- Describe and discuss the prevalence and characteristics of students at risk for school failure.
- List, describe, and be able to recommend adaptations and modifications to promote inclusion of students with other diverse learning needs.
- Describe the causes, issues in identification, and general classroom adaptations for students with ADHD and ADD.
- Analyze the prevalence, characteristics, issues in identification and general classroom adaptations for students who are gifted, creative, and talented.
- Discuss the prevalence, characteristics, issues in identification and general classroom adaptations for students from culturally and linguistically diverse backgrounds.
- Describe the prevalence, characteristics, issues in identification and general classroom adaptations for at-risk students.

Chapter Outline

I. STUDENTS SERVED UNDER SECTION 504
   A. Definitions, Prevalence, and Characteristics of Attention Deficit Hyperactivity Disorder
   B. Causes of ADHD
   C. Issues in Identification and Assessment of ADHD
   D. General Classroom Adaptations for Students with ADHD
      1. Behavioral interventions
      2. Cognitive-behavioral interventions
      3. Medications
      4. Combinations of behavioral, cognitive-behavioral, and medications

II. GIFTED, CREATIVE, AND TALENTED
   A. Definitions, Prevalence, and Characteristics of Gifted, Creative, and Talented
      1. Intellectually gifted
      2. Creative and talented
      3. Hidden gifted, creative, and talented
   B. Issues in Identification and Assessment of Gifted, Creative, and Talented
   C. General Classroom Accommodations for Students Who Are Gifted, Creative, and Talented
      1. Acceleration
      2. Enrichment
      3. Adapt instructional materials
      4. Adapt instructional and evaluation procedures

III. STUDENTS WHO ARE CULTURALLY AND LINGUISTICALLY DIVERSE

A. Prevalence, Definitions, and Characteristics of Cultural and Linguistic Diversity
    1. Cultural diversity
        a. Recognize the needs of students from multiracial families
    2. Develop a plan to address linguistic diversity
        a. Bilingual special education
B. Issues in Identification and Assessment
C. General Classroom Adaptations for Students from Culturally and Linguistically Diverse Backgrounds

IV. STUDENTS AT RISK
  A. Definitions, Prevalence, and Characteristics of Students at Risk
    1. Abused and neglected children
    2. Homeless children
    3. Alcohol and substance abuse
    4. Family Poverty
    5. Young, pregnant, and parents
    6. Warning signs for suicide or violence
  B. Issues in Identification and Assessment of Students at Risk
    1. Compensatory Education
  C. General Classroom Adaptations for Students at Risk

V. SUMMARY

Chapter Overview

- Students with diverse learning needs other than specific disability areas also are found in general education classes and can benefit greatly from teachers' assistance and attention.
- Students with diverse learning needs include those with attention deficit hyperactivity disorder, those who are gifted, talented, and creative, those from cultural and linguistically diverse backgrounds, and those at risk due to factors such as poverty, drug use, homelessness, teenage pregnancy, and child abuse and neglect.
- Students with attention deficit hyperactivity disorder may be served under Section 504 or IDEA. Adaptations for this group of individuals may include behavioral approaches, cognitive-behavioral training, medication, or combinations of the three.
- Students who are gifted, talented, or creative may be identified by a variety of methods, including test scores, behavioral descriptions, and qualitative/descriptive methods. Students who are gifted, talented, or creative may be served by acceleration programs, enrichment programs, or a combination of approaches.
- Students who are culturally or linguistically diverse may also present some special learning needs. Teachers should adopt a culturally sensitive, pluralistic approach that incorporates an awareness of cultural differences and their implications for learning.
- Because students who are culturally or linguistically diverse are often over represented in special education placements, teachers should be particularly careful when considering referral for special education. Unbiased testing, culturally sensitive behavioral expectations, and prereferral intervention strategies can help address this important issue.
- Factors considered to put students at risk for school failure include poverty, drug use, homelessness, teenage pregnancy, and child abuse and neglect. Contact and communication with students in question, their families, relevant school personnel, and community agencies can help address risk factors.

Multiple Choice

Select the statement that best answers each multiple choice question.

1. Students with ADHD who do not meet the requirements for services under IDEA may qualify under

    a. the Civil Rights Act for students with ADHD.
    b. Section 504 of the Vocational Rehabilitation Act.
    c. the Perkins Act.
    d. the Regular Education Initiative.

2. The major cause of ADHD has been identified as:

    a. Food additives
    b. Prenatal factors
    c. Neurological factors
    d. No single cause has been identified

3. According to the DSM-IV, which statement is false of ADHD?

    a. A child must be seven years of age.
    b. Symptomatic behaviors must persist for two years.
    c. Inattention and hyperactivity must be observed across settings.
    d. A child must display six out of nine characteristics.

4. Many reports indicate that _____ of the population is gifted and talented.

    a. 3–5%
    b. 8–12%
    c. 15–22%
    d. 25–34%

5. Which is NOT true of gifted, talented, or creative students?

    a. Come from all cultural and ethnic backgrounds
    b. May be underachievers
    c. May not score high on standardized tests
    d. All of the above are true

6. Asian Americans have been found to be

    a. overrepresented in special education.
    b. underrepresented in special education.
    c. equally represented in special education.
    d. overrepresented in some categories, but not others.

7. In the U.S. today, African Americans constitute:

   a. The largest minority group
   b. The fastest growing minority group
   c. The most diverse minority group
   d. All of the above

8. _____ refers to having students from diverse cultural groups learn to "fit in" with the dominant cultural group and leave their own culture behind.

   a. Cultural pluralism
   b. Assimilation
   c. Cultural adaptation
   d. Cultural transformation

9. Overrepresentation of some groups in special education may be due in part to:

   a. Cultural misunderstandings
   b. Unfamiliar examiners
   c. Inappropriate assessment procedures
   d. All of the above

10. Which of the following are resources for potential identification of students at risk?

   a. Special education personnel
   b. Psychologists
   c. Social workers
   d. All of the above

True or False

Determine if each statement is true or false.

1. Section 504 is an important part of the Individuals with Disabilities Education Act (IDEA).

   a. TRUE
   b. FALSE

2. Research has identified food additives and sugar as the most likely causes of ADHD.

   a. TRUE
   b. FALSE

3. Admitting a child to school early, or skipping grades, are some examples of acceleration programs.

   a. TRUE
   b. FALSE

4. Cultural pluralism refers to fostering of differing cultural groups within the school setting.

    a. TRUE
    b. FALSE

5. About half of homeless families are single mothers with an average of two to three children.

    a. TRUE
    b. FALSE

6. Giving a gifted child independent work on a topic of his or her interest is an example of enrichment.

    a. TRUE
    b. FALSE

7. Schools and teachers have the responsibility to report any signs of child abuse.

    a. TRUE
    b. FALSE

Short Answer/Essay

1. Jimmy is a student in your 1st grade general education class who has ADHD. He has trouble paying attention for more than 5 minutes at a time and can't stay in his seat more than 10 minutes. Even when he is in his seat he is bouncing around and watching everyone and everything except you. You are tired of yelling at him to pay attention and to sit down. Though he apologizes each time, you know he will do it again. The other students are able to ignore his actions better than you do. But his actions are affecting his grades since he has trouble finishing assignments and tests. He is also behind in most subjects because he can't seem to focus on what is going on in class.

    a. What are the strengths and weaknesses of this student?
    b. What are 3 possible modifications or interventions you could use to help Jimmy stay on task?

2. Historically, many people from cultures that migrated to the United States wanted to learn English and be assimilated into the majority culture. More recently there has been an emphasis on cultural pluralism where immigrants retain a strong connection with their ethnic heritage. Assimilation has been described as a "melting pot" while Cultural Pluralism has been described more as a "salad bowl." What are the advantages and disadvantages of each practice? What are some ways you may integrate multicultural education into your classroom?

3. Is it appropriate to have your gifted students tutor your students who are having difficulties? When might this be appropriate? When is it not appropriate?

4. We tend to judge risk factors from our own experiences or from general information. But with individual students it is best to find out more information before jumping to conclusions. What else would you need to know before assuming that these students were at risk of dropping out of school? Who would you ask? Should you interfere or is it best to wait to see if the situation improves?

- Justin tells you his father left the family and that his parents are getting a divorce.
- June has been absent a lot due to illness.
- Jasmine is hanging out with a group of students you believe are taking drugs.
- Jamie comes to school in dirty clothes and has poor personal hygiene.

For more activities related to chapter content, go to the Activities module in chapter 5 of the Companion Website at www.prenhall.com/mastropieri.
Activities

Chapter 6: Effective Instruction for All Students

Objectives

After studying this chapter, you should be able to:

- Describe the effective teaching variables, including planning for content coverage and delivering instruction.
- Identify the various types and levels of learning occurring across content areas.
- Identify strategies for maximizing academic engagement (time-on-task).
- Describe the teacher presentation (SCREAM) variables.
- Compare and contrast higher-level and lower-level questioning.
- Describe the use of practice activities to reinforce recall and comprehension.
- Describe the uses of formative evaluation and contrast with summative evaluation.
- Describe the PASS variables and their application to effective instruction in inclusive settings.

Chapter Outline

I. OVERVIEW OF EFFECTIVE INSTRUCTION
II. PLANNING CONTENT COVERAGE
    A.   Objectives
    B.   Scope and Sequence
    C.   Curriculum
    D.   Pacing
    E.   Planning for Learning
        1.   Types of learning
            a.   Discrimination learning
            b.   Factual learning
            c.   Rule learning
            d.   Procedural learning
            e.   Conceptual learning
            f.   Problem solving and critical thinking
        2.   Levels of learning
            a.   Acquisition and fluency
            b.   Application and generalization
        3.   Identification versus production
    F.   Addressing Learning Problems
III. USING EFFECTIVE TEACHING STRATEGIES
    A.   Maximizing Academic Engagement (Time on task)
        1.   Academic on-task behavior
            a.   On-task student behavior
            b.   On-task teacher behavior
        2.   Maximize academic engaged time
            a.   Streamline transition activities
            b.   Reduce inappropriate verbalizations
            c.   Minimize inappropriate social behavior
            d.   Use strategies for individual cases
    B.   Making Effective Teacher Presentations

　　　　1.　Structure
　　　　2.　Clarity
　　　　3.　Redundancy
　　　　4.　Enthusiasm
　　　　5.　Appropriate rate
　　　　6.　Maximized engagement
　　　　　　a.　Questioning
　　　　　　b.　Feedback
　　　　　　c.　Praise
　　C.　Monitoring Practice Activities
　　D.　Review
　　E.　Formative Evaluation
　　F.　Components of a Model Lesson
IV.　PROMOTING EFFECTIVE INCLUSIVE INSTRUCTION: THE PASS VARIABLES
　　A.　Prioritize Objectives
　　B.　Adapt Instruction, Materials, or the Environment
　　C.　Systematic Teaching, or the SCREAM Variables
　　D.　Systematic Evaluation
V.　SUMMARY

Chapter Overview

- Effective instruction variables are variables that have been shown to exert a positive effect on student achievement. These variables include planning for content coverage and using effective teaching strategies. Effective instruction variables have been demonstrated to be positively associated with achievement of all students in inclusive settings.
- Planning for content coverage is a critical component of teacher effectiveness. Teachers must consider carefully the role of objectives, scope and sequence, curriculum, pacing, and types and levels of learning.
- Types of learning include discrimination, factual, procedural, rule, conceptual, and problem solving/critical thinking. Levels of learning include acquisition, fluency, application, and generalization. Students can provide either identification or production responses. Consideration of types and levels of learning can be beneficial when planning instructional strategies.
- Effective teaching strategies include maximizing academic time-on-task, making effective teacher presentations, monitoring practice activities, review, and formative evaluation. All are critical components of effective teaching for all students.
- Effective teacher presentations use the SCREAM variables including structure, clarity, redundancy, enthusiasm, appropriate rate, and maximized engagement. Additionally, effectively used questioning, feedback, and praise are important contributors to student learning.
- Practice activities provide opportunities for students to solidify and apply their learning. Practice activities can include guided practice, in which teachers closely monitor student response, and independent practice, in which students work more independently. Frequent review allows for long-term learning.
- Formative evaluation refers to collecting student performance data throughout the course of instructional units, so that instructional decisions—such as increasing academic engaged time—can be made while instruction is still ongoing.
- A sample model of a lesson based on teacher effectiveness variables includes daily review, statement of objective, presentation of information, guided practice, independent practice, and formative evaluation. Model lessons are based on careful consideration of objectives, scope and

sequence of instruction, pacing, curriculum materials, and types/levels of learning expected for successful achievement of all students.

- The PASS variables stand for: Prioritize instruction, Adapt instruction, materials, or the environment, Systematic teaching using the SCREAM variables, and Systematic evaluation. The PASS variables provide a model for planning and delivering effective instruction in inclusive settings.

Multiple Choice

Select the statement that best answers each multiple choice question.

1. Which is an important "effective teaching" variable?

   a. Scope and sequence
   b. Delivery of instruction
   c. Practice activities
   d. All of the above

2. The curriculum should:

   a. Serve as an interface between the student and the learning objective
   b. Not determine instructional objectives
   c. Support and enhance the learning of instructional goals
   d. All of the above are true

3. Determining that one stimulus is either the same or different from another stimulus is

   a. factual learning.
   b. discrimination learning.
   c. conceptual learning.
   d. procedural learning.

4. Conceptual learning can be enhanced by:

   a. Multiple examples
   b. Provision of non-instances
   c. Statement and application of rules
   d. All of the above

5. The degree to which students are directly engaged physically and/or mentally in instruction is

   a. ADHD.
   b. on-task behavior.
   c. inattention and hyperactivity.
   d. off-task behavior.

6. The SCREAM variables include all except:

   a. Maximize engagement
   b. Enthusiasm
   c. Consistency
   d. Appropriate rate

7. Having all students choose or write down an answer before anyone responds is an example of

   a. overt responding.
   b. covert responding.
   c. individual responding.
   d. cooperative learning.

8. Questioning generally should be fast-paced for:

   a. Basic skills and basic facts
   b. Higher-order thinking
   c. Conceptual learning
   d. All of the above

9. The type of feedback delivered depends to some extent on

   a. the type of disability of the student.
   b. the type of curriculum being used.
   c. the type of response that has been given.
   d. the time of day.

10. In a model lesson, after daily review comes

   a. presentation of information.
   b. introductions.
   c. statement of purpose.
   d. eliciting prior knowledge.

True or False

Determine if each statement is true or false.

1. Monitoring the pace and instructional objectives are important considerations when planning content coverage.

   a. TRUE
   b. FALSE

2. Remembering the steps in solving long division problems is an example of conceptual learning.

   a. TRUE
   b. FALSE

3. A student transferring previously learned knowledge or skills to novel situations is known as generalization.

    a.   TRUE
    b.   FALSE

4. Formative evaluation occurs at the end of a school year to determine how much was learned during the year.

    a.   TRUE
    b.   FALSE

5. Identification criteria include pointing on a communication board, responding to matching, multiple-choice or true/false formats.

    a.   TRUE
    b.   FALSE

6. An example of a streamlined transition activity is when students have assigned places to quickly line up in an orderly fashion to go to the cafeteria.

    a.   TRUE
    b.   FALSE

7. Lower level questions are all that are appropriate for students with learning disabilities or mental retardation.

    a.   TRUE
    b.   FALSE

Short Answer/Essay

1. Jana moved with her family last year to the United States from Germany. Her English is not that of a native speaker, but she was taught English in Germany. Though she rarely speaks, when she does it is in a halting English. Jana is somewhat shy but she smiles a lot and has made one or two friends in your fifth grade class. She seems to understand well when you model activities or when you work with her individually. But whenever you teach the whole group she does not seem to understand or stay on-task. She does poorly on tests in all subjects. You are afraid she is at-risk for school failure.

    a.   What are the strengths and needs of the student?
    b.   What are 3 possible modifications or interventions you could use to help Jana to be successful in school?

2. What is wrong with the following objectives? A good objective includes content, conditions, and criteria. What could you add to each objective to improve it?

- Jasper will read a 100-word passage out of a fifth-grade science book.
- Jayleen will answer 4 out of 5 comprehension questions.
- After reading 5 math word problems involving subtraction with regrouping, Justin will do them.

3. Give an example for the SCREAM method. Explain what you would do for each of the following steps for a specific lesson.
- structure
- clarity
- redundancy
- enthusiasm
- appropriate rate
- maximized engagement

4. How can you maximize engagement through questioning? Give three examples of questions a teacher may ask about houses from around the world that would maximize student engagement.

5. Identify the type of learning (discrimination, factual, rule, procedural, conceptual, or problem solving) for each of the following examples:
- Writing an essay on the causes of the economic highs and lows
- Telling the numbers "6" and "9" apart
- Being able to identify an amphibian
- Learning names of types of rocks
- Learning how to add on a number line
- Learning to ask permission before getting out of seat

For more activities related to chapter content, go to the Activities module in chapter 6 of the Companion Website at www.prenhall.com/mastropieri.

Chapter 7: Improving Classroom Behavior and Social Skills

Objectives

After studying this chapter, you should be able to:

- Describe how to observe, record, and manage classroom behaviors.
- Identify effective classroom management strategies.
- Discuss less intensive classroom behavior strategies as well more formal management systems, and their implications for classroom management.
- Compare and contrast different methods of assessing social skills.
- Describe interventions to improve social skills.
- Discuss and evaluate important considerations of social skills training.

Chapter Outline

I.   MANAGING CLASSROOM BEHAVIOR
    A.   Understanding Behavior Problems
    B.   Observe and Record Classroom Behavior
        1.   Define behavior
        2.   Use observation and recording systems
        3.   Determine the context of behavior
        4.   Make graphic presentations of data
    C.   Use Effective Classroom Management Strategies
        1.   Establish a positive classroom atmosphere
            a.   Project a feeling, caring persona
            b.   Teach with sincerity and enthusiasm
        2.   Use less intensive strategies
            a.   Rules
            b.   Praise and ignoring
            c.   Proximity
            d.   Direct appeals
            e.   Use reprimands judiciously
            f.   Validate the student's feelings
        3.   Use more formal management systems
            a.   Reinforce positive behavior
            b.   Use punishment judiciously
            c.   Reward students with token systems
            d.   Train positive attributions
            e.   Post positive behavior
            f.   Use timeout for specific behavior problems
            g.   Use appropriate levels of timeout
            h.   Use debriefing procedures after timeout
            i.   Implement level systems
            j.   Use the "good behavior game"
            k.   Set up student contracting
            l.   Promote self-monitoring
            m.   Teach students self-instruction strategies

n. Train for generalization
D. Handling Confrontations
E. Life Span Interviewing/Life Spaces Crisis Intervention
F. Schoolwide Discipline Systems
1. Employing assertive discipline
2. Positive behavioral supports
II. TEACHING SOCIAL SKILLS
A. Social Skills Assessment
B. Train Students to Improve Social Skills
C. Choose Curriculum Materials Thoughtfully
D. Conduct On-the-Spot Training
E. Train for Generalization
F. Validate Treatments
III. SUMMARY

Chapter Overview

- Students misbehave in school for a variety of different reasons, such as gaining attention, gaining control, gaining retribution, or because of distrust of others.
- Much of students' behavior is controlled by the classroom environment.
- Classroom behaviors can be better observed, managed, and evaluated if they are operationalized and monitored by formal observation and recording systems, such as event recording, duration recording, time sampling, and interval recording.
- Establishing a positive classroom atmosphere is an important key to effective behavior management.
- Less intensive strategies, such as establishing rules, praise and ignoring, proximity, direct appeals, and reprimands, are helpful in maintaining appropriate classroom behavior.
- More formal management systems for effective behavior management include positive reinforcement, punishment, token systems, attribution training, public posting, timeout and level systems, the "Good Behavior Game," and contracting.
- Self-monitoring and self-instruction training is helpful in allowing students to take more awareness in, and control of, their own behavior.
- A variety of strategies can be used to deal effectively with confrontations and to prevent them from escalating.
- School-wide discipline systems have been effective in managing classroom behavior across entire school environments.
- Several methods exist for assessing social skills, including surveys, checklists, role play, and direct observation.
- Social skills are usually trained by modeling, reinforcement, shaping, and modeling-reinforcement. Several strategies can be effective in promoting generalization of social skills.
- The effectiveness of social skills training, like other academic and behavioral interventions, should be monitored and validated in individual cases.

Multiple Choice

Select the statement that best answers each multiple choice question.

1. One example of a "mistaken goal" (Dreikurs & Cassel, 1992) is

    a. concealing inadequacy.
    b. money or material gain.
    c. negative attributions.
    d. physical aggression.

2. Operationalized behaviors create behavioral objectives specifying:

    a. Why the behavior is wrong
    b. What the student could do in the future
    c. The criteria for acceptable performance
    d. All of the above

3. An "A-B-C" chart refers to:

    a. After, Before, Continuing.
    b. Antecedent, Behavior, Consequence.
    c. Alterable, Behavioral, Consecutive.
    d. Answering, Behaving, Co-existing.

4. When the observer tallies the number of times a particular behavior occurs, this is an example of

    a. event recording.
    b. duration recording.
    c. interval recording.
    d. time sampling.

5. The first and most important step in classroom management is

    a. establishing and enforcing rules that are understandable.
    b. maintaining consistency without "playing favorites".
    c. establishing and maintaining a positive, supportive classroom atmosphere.
    d. using praise and ignoring when they are most appropriate and reinforce behaviors.

6. _____ is a simple strategy of moving closer to students who are beginning to demonstrate inappropriate behavior.

    a. Direct appeal
    b. Proximity
    c. Effective monitoring
    d. Direct observation

7. Separation of the student from the routine classroom environment, usually for a violation of classroom rules, is referred to as

    a. corporal punishment.
    b. negative attribution.
    c. timeout.
    d. response cost.

8. Which is NOT a characteristic of a level system?

    a. Has been employed to improve transitions between special and regular education classrooms
    b. Students take more responsibility for their own behavior in the classroom
    c. Students receive privileges for demonstrating appropriate self-control
    d. All of the above are true

9. The Good Behavior Game

    a. is a role playing game to create positive behavior habits.
    b. is a contest to award the best individual behavior over a specified time period.
    c. rewards groups or teams of students for good behavior.
    d. is a type of level system for good behavior.

10. Which is NOT an advantage of school-wide discipline system?

    a. The consistency in rules can be beneficial to students who have difficulty adjusting to different standards or rules enforced in different classrooms
    b. The structured consistency can be beneficial to limit-seeking students
    c. School-wide discipline programs effectively address the specific needs of all individuals
    d. The same rules are enforced in the same way throughout the school system

True or False

Determine if each statement is true or false.

1. "Marco will exhibit on-task behavior in math class 85% of the time for four out of five consecutive days" is an operationalized behavior.

    a. TRUE
    b. FALSE

2. Tangible reinforcers include snacks, drinks, and praise.

    a. TRUE
    b. FALSE

3. Debriefing procedures typically occur after a specified period of timeout.

    a. TRUE
    b. FALSE

4. The most important thing to remember in handling a confrontation is to remain calm.

    a. TRUE
    b. FALSE

5. A student contract describes the rewards for exhibiting an agreed upon behavior.

    a. TRUE
    b. FALSE

6. Time out is an effective method that is often done in the hall outside the classroom.

    a. TRUE
    b. FALSE

7. Sociometric ratings are a direct measure of social skills.

    a. TRUE
    b. FALSE

Short Answer/Essay

1. You have a group of 5 boys in the back of your room that do not want to stay on task in 9th grade Algebra. Whenever the material gets a little difficult, one of them will make a joke and get the whole group laughing. Though you do not want to keep telling them to be quiet, they really disrupt the flow of your lessons and make it hard for other students to learn. The longer you ignore the lack of respect and disruptions, the more they escalate. You were told that one of the boys has an emotional disturbance but you are not sure if he is causing the problem or not. How do you gain control of your math class without having to spend all your time on classroom management?

    a. What are the strengths and needs of the students?
    b. What additional information would be helpful to assess to make better decisions about these students?
    c. What are 3 possible modifications or interventions you could use to help these students be successful and behave well in your math class?

2. Give an example for each of the following recording techniques:
- Event recording
- Duration recording
- Interval recording
- Time Sampling

3. When will proximity lessen or stop misbehavior in your classroom? What would you do if the misbehavior did not stop when you walked nearby?

4. If you find a child with no friends in your classroom is there anything you can do? Should you get involved? Why or why not?

For more activities related to chapter content, go to the Activities module in chapter 7 of the Companion Website at www.prenhall.com/mastropieri.

Chapter 8: Promoting Inclusion with Classroom Peers

Objectives

After studying this chapter, you should be able to:

- Gain an understanding of the advantages and potential limitations of cooperative learning.
- Compare the various types of cooperative group arrangements and activities.
- Compare and contrast the uses and features of cooperative learning and peer tutoring.
- Describe important teacher functions when employing cooperative learning.
- Gain an understanding of peer tutoring and the benefits to tutors and tutees.
- Describe and evaluate different types of peer tutoring programs (cross-age, same-age, & classwide).
- Describe the procedures for effectively employing a peer tutoring program.
- Compare and contrast peer assistance and peer tutoring.

Chapter Outline

I.   PROMOTING SOCIAL ACCEPTANCE
    A.   Circle of Friends
    B.   Special Friends
II.   PEER ASSISTANCE
    A.   What Is Peer Assistance?
    B.   Peer Training
        1.   Working with students with different types of disabilities
        2.   Peer social initiation
III. PEER TUTORING
    A.   Why Use Peer Tutoring?
    B.   Tutoring to Improve Academic Skills and Attitudes
        1.   Benefits to tutees
        2.   Benefits to tutors
    C.   Implementing a Tutoring Program
        1.   Cross-age tutoring
        2.   Same-age tutoring
    D.   Classwide Peer Tutoring
        1.   Peabody classwide peer tutoring in reading
        2.   Recommendations
                a.   Tutoring materials
                b.   Scheduling
                c.   Training
                d.   Interpersonal skills
        3.   Secondary Applications
IV.   COOPERATIVE LEARNING
    A.   Important Teacher Functions in Implementing Cooperative Learning
        1.   Create objectives
        2.   Determine group parameters
        3.   Explain goals, rules, and procedures
        4.   Monitor group activities

5. Evaluate individual and group efforts
   B. Integrating Students with Special Needs into Cooperative Groups
      1. Prepare students with special needs
      2. Prepare students without disabilities
   C. Types of Cooperative Group Arrangements
   D. Conflict Resolution
   E. Advantages and Limitations of Cooperative Learning
      1. Advantages
      2. Potential limitations
V. SUMMARY

Chapter Overview

- Peers can be taught a variety of strategies that involve students helping each other during classroom and school activities.
- Peer assistance can be used to promote inclusion of students with a variety of special needs.
- Circle of Friends and Special Friends are training programs that can promote classroom acceptance of students with disabilities or other special needs.
- Peer assistance refers to pairing students for the purpose of having one student available to assist another student when necessary.
- It is important to identify the situations that require peer assistance, appropriately train students, match peer assistants and buddies carefully, and monitor progress and modify as necessary.
- Tutoring is a powerful tool in improving classroom performance, and it can also be very helpful in addressing diverse learning needs in inclusive classrooms.
- Tutors and tutees both can gain academically and socially from tutoring interventions, although the procedures and outcomes should be carefully monitored.
- Classwide peer tutoring is one of the most highly recommended strategies for promoting achievement among diverse groups of learners.
- Cooperative learning is another strategy that can improve achievement and social integration of diverse learners.
- Cooperative learning interventions require specifying objectives, making placement decisions, explaining the task, monitoring effectiveness, and evaluating student achievement.
- A variety of formal and informal procedures for cooperative learning can be employed to address a variety of classroom situations.

Multiple Choice

Select the statement that best answers each multiple choice question.

1. Upper elementary students trained to interact with students with severe disabilities are an example of which program?

   a. Circle of Friends
   b. Special Friends
   c. Cross-age tutoring
   d. Cross-age mentoring

2. An important first consideration in preparing a peer assistance program is to

   a. determine the precise nature of the situation that requires assistance.
   b. identify students to be assigned peer assistants on the basis of their area of disability.
   c. consider the nature of the curriculum that will be undertaken.
   d. identify tutoring materials that reflect educational objectives.

3. Which is a step toward employing an effective peer tutoring program?

   a. Determine the content for tutoring material
   b. Devise a tutoring plan
   c. Monitor tutor roles and behavior
   d. All of the above

4. Peer social initiation is used for

   a. tutoring social skills.
   b. welcoming new students to the classroom.
   c. initiating students to classroom procedures.
   d. promoting social interaction with withdrawn children.

5. The most consistent benefits of peer tutoring are realized by

   a. tutors.
   b. tutees.
   c. younger students.
   d. older (secondary) students.

6. Which is true of cross-age tutoring?

   a. Tutoring roles alternate
   b. Tutors may keep a tutoring notebook
   c. Tutors and tutees come from the same class
   d. All of the above are true

7. How often are 35-minute classwide peer tutoring sessions recommended to be used?

   a. Once per day
   b. Once per week
   c. Three times per week
   d. Twice per day

8. In Peabody classwide peer tutoring, "Paragraph Shrinking," students

   a. predict what will happen next.
   b. say the main idea in 10 words or less.
   c. state what they learned first.
   d. read aloud for 5 minutes.

9. Which are appropriate considerations when planning cooperative groups?

   a. Choose groups that work well together
   b. Choose groups that are heterogeneous with respect to race, gender, or ability
   c. Use random assignment when assigning students to groups
   d. All of the above are important considerations

10. Which is NOT a recommended cooperative group activity?

   a. Small reading groups, with reader, recorder, checker.
   b. Students compete in groups to be group leader.
   c. Proofreading groups, where students proofread and critique each other's papers.
   d. Students work in groups to prepare for specific tests.

True or False

Determine if each statement is true or false.

1. One important use of peer assistance is in assisting students during emergency situations.

   a. TRUE
   b. FALSE

2. In cross-age tutoring, roles of tutor and tutee alternate.

   a. TRUE
   b. FALSE

3. Collaborative skills need not be taught as precisely as academic skills.

   a. TRUE
   b. FALSE

4. Peer mediation strategies can be used to manage conflict situations among peers.

   a. TRUE
   b. FALSE

5. Individual accountability is not necessary with cooperative learning.

   a. TRUE
   b. FALSE

6. Jigsaw is a cooperative learning method for putting together puzzles.

   a. TRUE
   b. FALSE

7. Peer tutoring is mainly used for increased socialization rather than instructional purposes.

    a. TRUE
    b. FALSE

Short Answer/Essay

1. Janice is a sweet girl in your 7th grade science class. She has mild mental retardation and has some awkward motor skills. She reads several years below her peers and she writes very slowly. She walks with a mild limp too. Janice is nice to others and tries very hard to follow your directions. In your science class you usually lecture then divide the class into cooperative groups for hands-on experiments. She usually can do the hands-on parts but is not able to write the lab reports. Janice is so slow at copying down the steps to the experiment that she rarely has time to complete the hands-on part in class. Due to her delays, no one wants to be in her cooperative group.

    a. What are the strengths and needs of the student?
    b. What are 3 possible modifications or interventions you could use to help Janice to be successful with her science lab?

2. Some research on cross-age tutoring matches older students with disabilities with younger students who do not have disabilities. Do you believe this would work? What do you see as possible pros and cons?

3. Under what circumstances would cooperative learning and peer-tutoring not be beneficial methodologies for your classroom?

4. The roles for some cooperative learning groups are as follows: reader, recorder, getter, starter. Which roles may inappropriate for the following students?
- A student with significant reading delays
- A student with difficulty writing
- A student with visual impairments
- A student who likes to throw materials around

For more activities related to chapter content, go to the Activities module in chapter 8 of the Companion Website at www.prenhall.com/mastropieri.

Chapter 9: Enhancing Motivation and Affect

Objectives

After studying this chapter, you should be able to:

- Describe the preconditions to improving motivation and affect in the classroom.
- Identify techniques for improving and enhancing student motivation and affect.
- Describe strategies for increasing self-efficacy.
- Demonstrate the uses of goal setting and attribution training.
- Discuss strategies for increasing students' personal investment in shared decision-making in the classroom.
- Identify and implement strategies to make learning more fun, exciting, and meaningful.
- Describe the uses of praise and reward to reinforce students' success in the classroom.
- Compare and contrast tangible and intangible rewards.

Chapter Outline

I. PRECONDITIONS FOR IMPROVING MOTIVATION AND AFFECT
   A. Create a Supportive, Organized Classroom Environment
      1. Elicit positive peer support
      2. Use statements that promote acceptance
   B. Ensure Materials Are of an Appropriate Difficulty Level
   C. Ensure that Tasks Are Meaningful
   D. Create Task-Oriented, Not Ego-Oriented Classrooms
II. TECHNIQUES FOR IMPROVING MOTIVATION AND AFFECT
   A. Raise Students' Self-Esteem
   B. Provide Opportunities to Increase Self-Efficacy
      1. Provide additional practice to reinforce prior knowledge
      2. Use ongoing assessment strategies
      3. Point out appropriate social models
      4. Provide positive support
      5. Avoid counterproductive statements
   C. Teach Students to Set Goals
      1. Establish goals and monitor progress
      2. Promote effort with contracts
      3. Encourage parent or family involvement
   D. Train Students to Use Positive Attributions
   E. Arrange Counseling Interventions When Needed
      1. Exercise care when handling serious affective disorders
   F. Increase Students' Personal Investment in the Classroom
      1. Share decision making for classroom procedures
      2. Solicit student feedback
   G. Make Learning More Fun and Enjoyable
      1. Make tasks more interesting
         a. Prepare more concrete, meaningful lessons
         b. Create cognitive conflict
         c. Use novel ways to engage students

                   d.   Develop competitive and gamelike activities
                   e.   Make use of cooperative learning
                   f.   Don't overdo motivational attempts
                   g.   Be enthusiastic!
        H.   Praise Students and Reward Their Efforts
              1.   Praise student effort
              2.   Use rewards to reinforce student success
                   a.   Avoid the overjustification effect
                   b.   Distinguish between rewards and "bribes"
                   c.   Set up conditions for rewards
                   d.   Set up performance criteria
                   e.   Develop appropriate performance criteria for students with special needs
                   f.   Use tangible and intangible rewards
                   g.   Justify fairness when necessary
III.   SUMMARY

Chapter Overview

- Motivation and affect are extremely important variables that can make the difference between success and failure in the classroom. Many students with special needs may benefit particularly from strategies to enhance motivation and affect.
- Before implementing specific strategies to enhance motivation and affect, ensure that the necessary preconditions have been met. These preconditions include creating a supportive, well-organized classroom environment; assigning tasks that are meaningful, concrete, relevant, and of the appropriate difficulty level; and creating task-oriented, rather than ego-oriented, classrooms, in which students are rewarded for effort and improvement, rather than for static variables such as "ability."
- Motivation and affect can be improved by engaging in practices to improve students' self-esteem, such as providing positive statements, assigning classroom responsibilities, and use of classroom peers.
- Self-efficacy is an important determiner of positive motivation and affect. Students succeed, and believe they will be successful, when provided with additional practice, advance organizers, appropriate social models, and positive support.
- Students' motivation and affect improves when they participate in setting goals for themselves and assist in monitoring their progress toward meeting these goals. Contracts and parent involvement can also contribute to personal goal-setting.
- Students feel more in control when they learn to attribute their classroom successes or failures to their own behaviors, such as appropriate effort, attitude, or academic/behavioral strategies. Students can appropriately take credit when they succeed, and identify strategies for improvement when they fail, when they make appropriate attributions.
- Students feel more ownership in the classroom when they participate in decision making involving classroom rules and procedures. Use a variety of techniques to receive input from students, and implement positive and helpful suggestions whenever possible.
- Students are more motivated to learn when learning is fun and interesting. Use a variety of approaches, media, gamelike activities, and peer interactions to prevent classroom learning from becoming monotonous and routine. Express personal enthusiasm in the subjects being covered, and teach with enthusiasm!
- Students are motivated to learn when their accomplishments are acknowledged and rewarded. Use positive feedback and praise frequently to demonstrate your positive regard for students'

accomplishments. Use rewards, in the form of prizes, privileges, or tokens, when needed to acknowledge achievement and maintain persistence of effort.

Multiple Choice

Select the statement that best answers each multiple choice question.

1. Which is NOT a precondition to increasing motivation and affect?

    a. Provide a supportive learning environment
    b. Create an environment where students compete for rewards
    c. Ensure instruction and tasks are at appropriate difficulty level
    d. All of the above are preconditions

2. Students are more motivated to learn when teachers:

    a. Lecture students on the importance of learning
    b. Use positive feedback
    c. Use strict discipline
    d. All of the above

3. In _____ students are evaluated with respect to previous performance and not against the performance of others

    a. task-oriented classrooms
    b. student-oriented classrooms
    c. ego-oriented classrooms
    d. none of the above

4. Goals should be:

    a. General and subjective
    b. Set at the highest possible level
    c. Realistic and attainable
    d. All of the above

5. Marcy believes the reason she failed history is because the teacher doesn't like her. This is an example of

    a. poor study skills.
    b. positive attributions.
    c. counterproductive effect.
    d. negative attributions.

6. Which of the following statements is NOT true:

    a. Enthusiasm is something teachers do and not something teachers are.
    b. Enthusiasm is frequently over-used.
    c. Enthusiams can be varied by individual teachers.
    d. All of the above are true.

7. One of the effective uses of praise is that praise:

    a. Should be used sparingly
    b. Should indicate the relation between effort and achievement.
    c. Should be delivered clearly and openly, so that other students will hear
    d. All of the above are effective uses of praise

8. Cognitive conflict refers to

    a. social conflict due to misunderstandings.
    b. misapplication of procedures over several successive events.
    c. misunderstandings about test questions or homework instructions.
    d. situations that are not easily predictable or explainable at first.

9. Overjustification occurs when

    a. interest is low and rewards are very tangible.
    b. interest is high and rewards are very tangible.
    c. interest is high and rewards are intrinsic.
    d. interest is low and rewards are low.

10. According to Richards La Voie, fairness means

    a. everyone is treated the same.
    b. everyone is treated the way he or she prefers.
    c. everyone is treated according to individual needs.
    d. all have equal rights under law.

True or False

Determine if each statement is true or false.

1. Intrinsic motivation refers to the participation in an activity in anticipation of an external reward.

    a. TRUE
    b. FALSE

2. Common external rewards for school children are pencils, stickers and treats.

    a. TRUE
    b. FALSE

3. Students with special needs are generally more motivated to achieve in ego-oriented classrooms.

    a. TRUE
    b. FALSE

4. "I passed the test because I got lucky" is an example of a negative attribution.

   a. TRUE
   b. FALSE

5. "I failed the test because I did not study" is an example of a negative attribution.

   a. TRUE
   b. FALSE

6. Teacher enthusiasm variables include use of a varied choice of words.

   a. TRUE
   b. FALSE

7. Regardless of disability area, all students with special needs enjoy novelty in their environments.

   a. TRUE
   b. FALSE

Short Answer/Essay

1. You have been told that Julian is a gifted student, so you were excited to get him in your 8th grade English class. Unfortunately, he spends most of the time making snide comments under his breath to the other students to get a laugh at your expense. When you confront him, he does stop, but then draws pictures, reads novels, or engages in an off-task activity. When you ask him to show you his work he says he will do it later. His work is passable when he gets around to doing it, but you think he is bored and completely unmotivated. You can't raise the level of teaching in your class since the majority of your students are having trouble keeping up with the pace you set. How do you teach your class, but also meet Julian's needs?

   - What are the strengths and weaknesses of the student?
   - What additional information would be helpful to assess to make better decisions about this student?
   - What are 3 possible modifications or interventions you could use to help Julian to be successful in your English class?

2. What are two examples of educational games you can play in your classroom to motivate your students?

3. Students are motivated when given appropriate levels of work. What does that mean? How do students behave when the work it too easy? How do students behave when the work it too difficult?

4. Praise is effective if it is specific to the situation. It is also better when it is sincere. Which of the following are effective examples of praise? Can you rewrite the ineffective examples to be more effective?

- I like the colors you are using in that painting.
- Wow, you are a great athlete!
- You look pretty today.
- That is a nice outfit you are wearing.
- When you had all of the visual aids with your book report, it really made it interesting.
- You did nice work on the test.
- Your story was very well written and it kept my interest until the end. I could not wait to see what happened next!
- You are going to be the next Einstein!

For more activities related to chapter content, go to the Activities module in chapter 9 of the Companion Website at www.prenhall.com/mastropieri.

Chapter 10: Improving Attention and Memory

Objectives

After studying this chapter, you should be able to:

- Describe preconditions for improving attention in the classroom.
- Describe and analyze extreme cases of attention deficits and the effects of stimulant medications.
- Understand the importance of memory and attention for students with special needs to school success.
- Describe preconditions and the various strategies for improving memory for students with special needs.
- Design and implement strategies to enhance meaning and concreteness of instruction.
- Understand various ways to promote active learning and increase practice through clustering, organization, and elaboration.
- Describe, create, and apply mnemonic strategies (keyword, pegword, and letter strategies) to improve and enhance memory.

Chapter Outline

I. ATTENTION
    A. Attention and Students with Special Needs
    B. Strategies for Improving Attention
        1. Preconditions
        2. Direct appeal
        3. Proximity
        4. Break up activities
        5. Allow sufficient movement
        6. Provide student activities
        7. Use classroom peers to promote attention
        8. Provide reinforcement for attention
        9. Teach self-recording strategies
    C. Basic skills problems
    D. Extreme cases of attention deficits
    E. Intensive teacher-led instruction
    F. Stimulant medication
        1. Autism
II. MEMORY
    A. Aspects of Memory
    B. Memory and Students with Special Needs
    C. Preconditions for Improving Memory
    D. Strategies for Improving Memory
        1. Develop "metamemory"
        2. Use external memory
        3. Enhance meaningfulness
        4. Use of concrete examples, pictures, or imagery
            a. Video presentations
            b. Illustrations
            c. Imagery

<ol start="5">
<li>Minimize interfering information</li>
<li>Use enactments and manipulation
  <ol type="a">
    <li>Symbolic enactments</li>
  </ol>
</li>
<li>Promote active learning</li>
<li>Increase practice</li>
<li>Clustering and organization</li>
<li>Elaboration</li>
</ol>

E. Improve Memory with Mnemonic Techniques

<ol>
<li>Keyword strategies
  <ol type="a">
    <li>"Reconstructive elaborations"</li>
  </ol>
</li>
<li>Pegword strategies</li>
<li>Letter strategies</li>
<li>Creating mnemonic pictures</li>
<li>Combining mnemonic strategies with other classroom activities</li>
<li>Other types of mnemonics</li>
</ol>

III. SUMMARY

Chapter Overview

- Attention and memory are two important psychological processes necessary for success in school. Being able to attend to and remember academic content is often a problem for many students with special needs. However, research has uncovered many successful strategies for enhancing attention and memory.
- Effective teaching, including using the teacher planning and presentation variables, can help all students pay more attention in class.
- Simple strategies for increasing attention include asking students directly to try to pay attention better, or moving closer to the student who struggles to attend.
- Breaking activities into smaller segments, alternating among various types of class activities, allowing opportunities for movement, using reinforcement, and teaching self-recording may also help improve attending.
- Peer assistance can be used to promote attention of students with a variety of special needs. Reinforcement of attention and teaching self-recording strategies can also be effective.
- Meeting the preconditions for improving memory may help many students remember better. These preconditions include promoting attention, motivation, and positive attitudes.
- Teaching students metacognitive awareness strategies helps promote better memory strategies for all students.
- Using pictures, enhancing meaningfulness, using activities, providing sufficient practice, and promoting active learning all help promote better memory for students with disabilities.
- Using mnemonic strategies such as the keyword method, the pegword method, and letter strategies helps promote learning of unfamiliar content.

Multiple Choice

Select the statement that best answers each multiple choice question.

1. Students in which disability category may exhibit difficulties sustaining attention?

    a. Students with learning disabilities
    b. Students with mental retardation
    c. Students with physical or sensory impairments
    d. All of the above

2. _____ is memory of facts and concepts about the world, known independently of one's personal experiences.

    a. Semantic memory
    b. Short-term memory
    c. Working memory
    d. Episodic memory

3. _____ is a term that defines the metacognitive process of knowing about memory.

    a. Episodic memory
    b. Metamemory
    c. Cognition
    d. Meta-analysis

4. Creating a mental picture to assist in memory is an example of

    a. metamemory.
    b. imagery.
    c. external memory.
    d. working memory.

5. An example of an enactment is:

    a. Creating a poem from information to be remembered
    b. Acting out information, as in a play or skit
    c. Doing a relevant activity, rather than reading or hearing about the same information
    d. All of the above are enactments

6. The keyword method can be used effectively for remembering:

    a. Vocabulary words
    b. People and their accomplishments
    c. Abstract terminology
    d. All of the above

7. _____ are rhyming words for numbers, and are useful in learning numbered or ordered information.

    a. Pegword strategies
    b. Keyword strategies
    c. Letter strategies
    d. All of the above

8. The HOMES strategy to prompt recall of the names of the Great Lakes is an example of

    a. mimetic reconstructions.
    b. keyword strategy.
    c. pegword strategy.
    d. letter strategy.

9. A good pegword for seven is:

    a. A picture of seven pencils or other objects
    b. Heaven
    c. Several
    d. All of the above could be used as pegwords

10. Using the phrase "My Dear Aunt Sally" to remember procedures in mathematics is an example of a(n)

    a. acrostic.
    b. acronym.
    c. pegword.
    d. reconstructive elaboration.

True or False

Determine if each statement is true or false.

1. Directly asking students to pay attention can improve their attention.

    a. TRUE
    b. FALSE

2. Self-recording systems for attending often employ a timer.

    a. TRUE
    b. FALSE

3. Self-monitoring of attention is usually more effective than self-monitoring of performance.

    a. TRUE
    b. FALSE

4. Clustering refers to grouping different types of information by category, and then rehearsing the information.

    a. TRUE
    b. FALSE

5. A good keyword for "celebrate" could be "party."

    a. TRUE
    b. FALSE

6. Pegwords are rhyming words used to represent numbers, such as "hive" for five.

    a. TRUE
    b. FALSE

7. Visual aides can assist a student's memory of a concept.

    a. TRUE
    b. FALSE

Short Answer/Essay

1. Jezebel is a student in your second grade class with moderate mental retardation. She is not able to read words, but she does know how to identify letters and her numbers most of the time. You are working with the special education teacher on an alternative curriculum for her. One of the IEP objectives states that she will be able to count up to 9 items and then point to the corresponding number. You are having her count pictures on a worksheet then circle the correct number. Jezebel can only do it with assistance. What else can you try to help improve her memory?

    a. What are the strengths and needs of the student?
    b. What are 3 possible modifications or interventions you could use to help Jezebel to be successful on the IEP objective?

2. How do you transfer information from short-term memory to long-term memory? Give examples of how you remember a new phone number that you do not want to have to look up.

3. What is a mnemonic you have used in the past? Can you make one up on the spot? For example, how do you remember which is the symbol for greater than (>) or less than (<)? Most people use a mnemonic device. Can you devise a mnemonic for how to spell the state that you live in?

4. What factors impact memory? If you are tired, how good is your memory? What happens to a student's memory if they are upset, or hungry, or distracted by a classmate?

For more activities related to chapter content, go to the Activities module in chapter 10 of the Companion Website at www.prenhall.com/mastropieri.

Chapter 11: Teaching Study Skills

Objectives

After studying this chapter, you should be able to:

- Develop understanding of tools to develop independent learners and develop personal organizational skills.
- Identify ways to clearly state class expectations toward successful completion of homework.
- Define the purpose, requisite skills, and various strategies to practice effective listening skills.
- Identify and demonstrate understanding of various notetaking skills and strategies.
- Demonstrate familiarity with various library resources and reference skills necessary to successfully complete a report or project.
- Describe and apply strategies for assisting students with disabilities to prepare reports and projects.

Chapter Outline

I. TOOLS TO DEVELOP INDEPENDENT LEARNERS
    A. Help Students Develop Personal Organizational Skills
        1. Post and review class and time schedules
            a. How to start
            b. Don't forget lockers
            c. Clearly post and review schedule changes
        2. Daily, weekly, monthly planners, and planning
        3. Task analysis
        4. Homework
            a. Clearly state class expectations
            b. Plan for special problems
            c. Cooperative homework teams
            d. Assignment completion strategy
    B. Promote Listening Skills
        1. Define the purpose
        2. Requisite listening skills
        3. Teach listening skills
            a. Adjust lectures
        4. Plan for special problems
    C. Note Taking
        1. Define the purpose
        2. Teach note-taking skills and strategies
            a. Be prepared
            b. Teach how to write short summaries
            c. Ask questions for clarification
            d. Teach abbreviations
            e. Use specific formats for note taking
            f. Teach speed and accuracy techniques
            g. Teach students how to study using notes
            h. The LINKS strategy

                i.   The AWARE strategy
                j.   The three and five R's strategies
        3.   Address special problems

II.   RESEARCH AND REFERENCE SKILLS
     A.   Teach Library Skills
        1.   Reference books
        2.   Databases
        3.   Library catalogs
        4.   Computerized literature searches
            a.   Computerized searches of encyclopedias
            b.   Use of search engines on the World Wide Web
        5.   Plan for special problems
     B.   Help Students Prepare Reports and Projects
        1.   Define the writing task
            a.   Select topic
        2.   Develop a writing plan
        3.   Brainstorm ideas
        4.   Find and collect information
        5.   Organize ideas and information
        6.   Write draft of paper
        7.   Obtain feedback on draft
        8.   Revise and rewrite
        9.   Proof and edit final version
        10.   Teach the entire process

III.   SUMMARY

Chapter Overview

- Students with disabilities and those at risk for failure in school benefit from very explicit instruction and practice in study skills.
- Personal organization skills, such as knowing about class times and schedules, using assignment notebooks and monthly planners, and organizing homework, are important for success in school and can be effectively taught to students with special needs.
- Direct teaching of listening skills helps students with special needs be prepared to learn information presented orally in school.
- Teaching students ways to take notes, including writing short summaries, abbreviations, using specific notetaking formats, and specific notetaking strategies, facilitates learning from lectures and presentations.
- Practice and instruction using the library, including use of reference materials, indices, computerized literature searches, use of the World Wide Web, and use of Internet search engines, assists students with special needs in learning how to search for and locate resources for schoolwork.
- Direct instruction on how to write a research paper, including selecting topics, searching for information, organizing information, writing and editing first drafts, and preparing final versions, is essential for most students with special needs.

Multiple Choice

Select the statement that best answers each multiple choice question.

1. A good way to help students keep track of long-term and short-term assignments is:

    a. Lecture on the importance of planning
    b. Demonstrate how to use daily planners
    c. Provide negative consequences for neglecting assignments
    d. None of the above

2. The process of taking a large task or assignment and breaking it into smaller tasks is known as

    a. long-term planning.
    b. positive attributions.
    c. task analysis.
    d. concept analysis.

3. When assigning homework, it is helpful to:

    a. Explain the purpose of the assignment
    b. Describe necessary materials
    c. Coordinate assignments with other teachers
    d. All of the above

4. Homework should not be assigned unless:

    a. Other teachers assign homework and yours is of equal length
    b. Students possess skills and knowledge to complete it independently
    c. Students request homework and will have parental supervision
    d. All of the above

5. The LINKS strategy is intended to help students with

    a. homework.
    b. note taking.
    c. assignments.
    d. reports.

6. The 'W' in the AWARE strategy stands for:

    a. avoid Wrong conclusions.
    b. Write quickly.
    c. Within 10 minutes, note down important headings.
    d. What is the point of the lecture.

7. The difference between the three-R and five-R strategies is that the five-R strategy includes

    a. more preparation steps.
    b. steps for questioning.
    c. more after-lecture studying steps.
    d. self-questioning strategies.

8. If a note taker is too slow, one appropriate strategy is:

    a. Excuse the student from class
    b. Provide a basic outline as a handout
    c. Do not require notetaking
    d. All of the above

9. To help students decide what to write in note taking:

    a. Organize lecture logically
    b. Write key points on board or overhead as you lecture
    c. Provide guided notes as handouts for students
    d. All of the above

10. INSPECT is a proofreading strategy to be used with

    a. word processors.
    b. cooperative learning groups.
    c. book reports.
    d. essays.

True or False

Determine if each statement is true or false.

1. Many students with disabilities lack effective study and learning strategies.

    a. TRUE
    b. FALSE

2. Task analysis is a strategy for determining how important a task is.

    a. TRUE
    b. FALSE

3. Self-monitoring sheets can be helpful in meeting class work expectations.

    a. TRUE
    b. FALSE

4. The first important listening skill is "determine the purpose."

    a. TRUE
    b. FALSE

5. One way to improve your students' listening skills is to adjust your lecture to include key words or cues.

    a. TRUE
    b. FALSE

6. "Partial outline" means that students complete outlines for only the first part of the teacher presentation.

    a. TRUE
    b. FALSE

7. There is no best way to make a study outline for students with special needs.

    a. TRUE
    b. FALSE

Short Answer/Essay

1. You teach a high school history class. John has average intelligence but also has a hearing impairment that prevents him from taking good notes in your class. He reads from the book well, but you like to test students from the discussions and lectures as well. He has a hearing aid and he sits in the front row. But he still misses a lot of what you say since you walk around the room when lecturing.

    a. What are the strengths and needs of the student?
    b. What are 3 possible modifications or interventions you could use to help John to be successful taking notes?

2. Why might you need to teach students how to use a table of contents or a glossary? How will these skills help all of your students, especially students with learning disabilities?

3. There is research evidence that individuals who learn test-taking strategies do better on tests. What test taking strategies do you use for tests? Which of these would be helpful for your students to learn, especially your students with test-taking problems?

4. Write a task analysis for looking up a word in a dictionary. How many steps does it take? What prerequisite skills do you assume the student has already?

For more activities related to chapter content, go to the Activities module in chapter 11 of the Companion Website at www.prenhall.com/mastropieri.

Chapter 12: Assessment

Objectives

After studying this chapter, you should be able to:

- Describe the use of norm-referenced tests, competency-based assessments, teacher-made tests, and criterion-referenced tests in inclusive settings.
- Identify and implement strategies to modify test formats to meet the needs of students with disabilities.
- Compare and contrast curriculum-based measurement, performance assessment, and portfolio assessments, and their applications for students with special needs.
- Describe specific test-taking strategies for taking standardized tests, and explain how these strategies can be taught.
- Design and implement strategies for taking teacher-made tests such as multiple choice, true-false, matching, and essay tests.
- Identify procedures and rationales for modifying grading and scoring of tests for students with special needs.

Chapter Outline

I. TYPES OF TESTS
II. ADAPTING TESTS FOR STUDENTS WITH SPECIAL NEEDS
    A. Norm-Referenced Tests
        1. Use test modifications
        2. Use individually administered tests
        3. Teach test-taking skills
        4. Increase motivation
        5. Improve examiner familiarity
        6. Request modifications for college entrance exams
    B. Adapt Competency-Based and Statewide Assessments
        1. Use test modifications or accommodations
        2. Use alternate assessments
        3. Request modifications on GED tests
    C. Adapt Teacher-Made and Criterion-Referenced Tests
        1. Modify tests
            a. Modify test formats.
            b. True–false items
            c. Multiple-choice items
            d. Matching items
            e. Sentence completion items
            f. Essay questions
        2. Modify scoring procedures
III. USING CURRICULUM-BASED MEASUREMENT
IV. USING PERFORMANCE ASSESSMENT
V. USING PORTFOLIO ASSESSMENT
    A. Applications for Students with Special Needs
VI. TEACHING TEST-TAKING SKILLS
    A. General Preparation Strategies
    B. Strategies for Standardized Tests

1. Teach general strategies
   a. Separate answer sheets
   b. Use elimination strategies
   c. Guess when appropriate
   d. Use time wisely
C. Teach Specific Strategies for Standardized Tests
   1. Reading comprehension subtests
   2. Decoding subtest strategies
   3. Mathematics computation subtests
      a. Mathematics concepts subtests
   4. Math problem-solving subtests
   5. Science and social studies subtests
D. Teacher-Made Tests
   1. Objective tests
   2. Written tests
      a. Sentence completion items
      b. Short-answer items
      c. Essay questions
   3. Performance tests
E. Other Test-Taking Strategies
VII. GRADING AND SCORING
A. Report Card Grades
   1. Modify grading procedures
B. SUMMARY

Chapter Overview

- Many types of tests are used in education; however, all tests must be reliable and valid to be useful.
- Norm-referenced testing compares the score of an individual with the scores of other students in a standardization sample.
- Modifications in standardized tests or administration procedures may detract from the validity of the test. However, such modifications as teaching test-taking skills, enhancing motivation, and enhancing examiner familiarity may improve test validity without compromising standardization.
- Competency-based and state-wide testing assesses the skill levels of students and is being used more often in schools. Some modifications in these tests may be appropriate for students with special needs.
- Teacher-made tests can be modified to obtain a clearer picture of student performance without detracting from the test itself. Modifications can be applied to a wide variety of test formats.
- Curriculum-based measurement is an excellent means of documenting the progress of all students, including students with disabilities or other special needs. Curriculum-based measurement allows the teacher to make instructional decisions as instruction is going on.
- Performance assessment serves to evaluate student competence with respect to particular instructional units. Because it focuses more on doing than writing or speaking, it may be particularly suited for diverse classrooms.
- Portfolio assessment is an ongoing means for obtaining information from student products and other sources. It is a particularly useful form of assessment that also has direct applications to some students with disabilities.

- Explicit instruction on general strategies to improve test performance, such as academic preparation, physical preparation, reducing anxieties, and increasing motivation, can improve the test performance of students with special needs.
- General strategies for improving standardized test performance include using separate answer sheets, using time wisely, elimination, and guessing strategies. Test-taking strategies for specific types of subtests can also improve standardized test performance.
- Test-taking strategies for teacher-made tests include strategies for taking objective tests, written tests, including fill-in-the-blank, short-answer, and essay tests.
- Some other test-taking strategies, such as SNOW, SCORER, PIRATES, and ANSWER, have been successfully taught to students with special needs and have improved their performance.
- Modifications can be made in grading and scoring the work of students with special needs. These modifications can be applied on report card grades, homework, and seatwork.

Multiple Choice

Select the statement that best answers each multiple choice question.

1. Which assessment is a collection of students' products and other relevant information collected over time?

   a. Performance assessment
   b. Curriculum-based measurement
   c. Portfolio assessment
   d. Curriculum-based assessment

2. Which is a testing modification for norm-referenced tests?

   a. Changing the setting
   b. Testing individually
   c. Extend time limits
   d. All of the above

3. "Matching" test formats can be made easier for students with special needs to use by:

   a. Increasing the number of items
   b. Matching the number of items in each column
   c. Placing the test on several pages
   d. Writing in clues to help eliminate guessing

4. Curriculum-based measurement can be very effective in improving the achievement of

   a. students with disabilities.
   b. all low-achieving students.
   c. normally-achieving students.
   d. all students in inclusive classrooms.

5. Performance assessment is particularly useful for students with disabilities because:

    a. The standards are lower than on other assessments
    b. Students can receive help from others or their teachers
    c. Students can demonstrate what they know on "real" tasks
    d. All of the above

6. General preparation strategies for tests include which of the following:

    a. Academic preparation
    b. Physical preparation
    c. Reducing test anxiety
    d. All of the above

7. Elimination strategies involve removing

    a. difficult questions at first.
    b. answer choices known not to be correct.
    c. superfluous answer choices during test construction.
    d. less heavily-weighted test items.

8. Which is an effective strategy for math computation subtests?

    a. Divide scratch paper in quarters on each side and compute
    b. Rewrite problem into comfortable format
    c. Practice checking answers on scratch paper
    d. All of the above

9. Words such as "always" and "never," which should be considered carefully when taking a test, are referred to as

    a. command words.
    b. clue words.
    c. specific determiners.
    d. stem options.

10. This strategy facilitates essay test performance.

    a. ANSWER
    b. SCORER
    c. PIRATES
    d. INSPECT

True or False

Determine if each statement is true or false.

1. Curriculum-based assessment could include any procedure that evaluates student performance in relation to the school curriculum.

    a. TRUE
    b. FALSE

2. Reliability and validity are not necessary for some types of tests.

    a. TRUE
    b. FALSE

3. Deviations from standard administration procedures do not usually limit the usefulness of the test.

    a. TRUE
    b. FALSE

4. It is ethical to modify tests for students with disabilities as long as you offer the same modifications to students without disabilities

    a. TRUE
    b. FALSE

5. Essay questions can not easily be modified, since the student does most of the writing.

    a. TRUE
    b. FALSE

6. One way of modifying grading for students with disabilities is to base the grading on goals and objectives in the IEP.

    a. TRUE
    b. FALSE

7. The best way to modify grades for students with disabilities is to inflate them so they do not feel badly.

    a. TRUE
    b. FALSE

Short Answer/Essay

1. Janie is a student who has cerebral palsy. She has average cognition but cannot write well or speak well. She likes to interact with others and has some friends in the class who seem to understand her. Janie is able to point but only if the object or area is larger than allowed by regular worksheets. She has a great attitude and works hard but you do not always know what she understands. Janie needs to take tests in

several subjects this week. You hope she does well on them, but you need to make sure she can answer the questions.

- What are the strengths and weaknesses of the student?
- What additional information would be helpful to assess to make better decisions about this student?
- What are 3 possible modifications or interventions you could use to help Janie to be successful on tests?

2. What would be the best way to assess the following student skills or knowledge?
- Focusing a microscope
- Basic multiplication facts
- Writing a paragraph
- Eligibility for special education

3. What activities can a teacher do to improve her students' with disabilities' performance on a norm-referenced test?

4. How would you modify the following test formats?
- Essay test for a student who is blind
- Spelling test for a student who has a significant hearing loss

For more activities related to chapter content, go to the Activities module in chapter 12 of the Companion Website at www.prenhall.com/mastropieri.

Chapter 13: Literacy

Objectives

After studying this chapter, you should be able to:

- Understand considerations and adaptive approaches to basal textbooks, whole language, reading recovery, direct instruction, and code emphasis approaches.
- Describe adaptations for promoting word identification, including phonemic awareness, phonics, structural analysis, and basic sight words.
- Understand adaptations and technological advances to promote reading fluency, including repeated readings, curriculum-based measurement, and various computer programs.
- Design and implement strategies for teaching reading comprehension in inclusive settings.
- Describe and implement instructional and technological adaptations for written expression.
- Implement instructional strategies to enhance and improve spelling for students in inclusive settings.
- Describe and implement effective composition strategies, such as self-regulation and self-instruction.

Chapter Outline

I. READING
   A. Using Basal Textbooks
      1. Developing reading skills using basals
      2. Adapting basal approaches
   B. The Whole Language Approach
      1. Adapting whole language approaches
   C. Reading Recovery
   D. Direct Instruction and Code Emphasis
      1. Considerations and adaptations
   E. Adaptations for Promoting Word Identification
      1. Phonemic awareness
      2. Phonics
      3. Structural analysis
      4. Basic sight vocabulary
   F. Adaptations for Promoting Reading Fluency
      1. Repeated readings
      2. Curriculum-based measurement
      3. Classwide peer tutoring
      4. Computer programs
   G. Technological Adaptations to Promote Reading
II. READING COMPREHENSION
   A. Strategies for Teaching Reading Comprehension in Inclusive Settings
      1. Use basic skills and reinforcement strategies
      2. Create text enhancements
      3. Teach specific reading comprehension strategies
         a. Activate prior knowledge
         b. Promote self-generated questions
         c. Summarize and paraphrase

           d.   Story maps

           e.   Reciprocal teaching

    B.   Instructional Adaptations that Foster Reading Comprehension

    C.   Secondary Applications

III.   WRITTEN EXPRESSION

    A.   Handwriting

        1.   Incorporate self-regulation and self-instructional strategies

        2.   Manuscript vs. cursive writing

        3.   Technological adaptations

    B.   Spelling

        1.   Select words from reading and writing activities

        2.   Self-instructional and self-monitoring strategies

        3.   Self-questioning

        4.   Cover–copy–compare or study-test-study

        5.   Curriculum and software

        6.   Adapt spelling objectives

    C.   Written Communication

        1.   Self-regulation and self-instructional writing strategies

           a.   How to identify story grammar

           b.   Choose effective composition strategies

        2.   Thinking about writing

        3.   Essays using computers

        4.   Support for research reports

        5.   Proofreading that integrates computer and strategy use

        6.   Adapt instruction to overcome mechanical obstacles

        7.   Curriculum materials

IV.   SUMMARY

Chapter Overview

- Many approaches exist for teaching students to read. Many students with reading disabilities lack phonemic awareness or phonics skills and overuse context cues when trying to read. Teachers should select reading programs that consider these need areas.
- Phonemic awareness is the understanding that words are composed of smaller speech sounds (phonemes). Systematic instruction in phonemic awareness can be beneficial for students who lack this understanding.
- Sequenced phonics instruction is also usually helpful for students with reading problems. Phonics instruction is most helpful when it is used in conjunction with other reading and language arts activities, focuses on reading words rather than learning rules, and includes learning onsets and rimes.
- Reading comprehension strategies can be employed before, during, or after reading. These strategies include basic skills instruction and text enhancements. Self-monitoring and self-questioning strategies are among the most effective reading comprehension strategies.
- Handwriting problems can be addressed by providing models and sufficient practice, using behavioral techniques, and teaching self-regulation and self-instruction strategies.
- A variety of strategies have been described for improving problem spelling performance. These include using the appropriate difficulty level, providing additional practice, mnemonic strategies, and self-instructional and self-monitoring strategies.
- Written communication difficulties can be addressed by using collaborative peer groups, teaching self-regulation and self-instruction strategies, using story grammar, and effective specific

composition strategies. Adapting instruction for students' special needs can promote more inclusive classroom environments.

Multiple Choice

Select the statement that best answers each multiple choice question.

1. Snider (1997) states that some estimate that as many as _____ of students do not discover sound-symbol relationships on their own without explicit instruction.

    a. 10%
    b. 25%
    c. 38%
    d. 52%

2. _____ has been defined as "the method of using sounds of a language when teaching people to read" (Fischer, 1993, p. 1).

    a. Language experience
    b. Linguistics
    c. Phonics
    d. Whole language

3. Which statement is FALSE regarding an exemplary phonics program?

    a. Builds on students' prior knowledge about how print works
    b. Emphasizes memorizing rules, before reading words
    c. Is integrated within a reading and language arts program
    d. Emphasizes development of fluency building word recognition skills

4. _____ refers to the ability to examine structures of words and break them into pronounceable syllables.

    a. Phonological analysis
    b. Structural analysis
    c. Phonics structures
    d. Structural phonemics

5. _____ are irregular words that are used frequently at various grade levels.

    a. Sight words
    b. Phonemes
    c. Mnemonics
    d. All of the above

6. Timing students' oral reading several days a week and charting their performance over extended time periods is an example of

    a. curriculum-based assessment.
    b. repeated readings.
    c. curriculum-based measurement.
    d. criterion-referenced assessment.

7. Which of the following is a strategy to activate prior knowledge?

    a. TELLS fact or fiction
    b. Story maps
    c. Reciprocal teaching
    d. All of the above

8. Which of the following is an example of a self-generated question?

    a. What are you studying the passage for?
    b. Find the main idea in the paragraph and underline it/them
    c. Learn the answer to your question
    d. All of the above

9. The peer-questioning activity, "Sharing Chair," is intended to help students:

    a. Correct their errors
    b. Expand their ideas
    c. Brainstorm new topics
    d. All the above

10. The TREE strategy is intended to help students

    a. remember details.
    b. learning spelling words.
    c. plan their essays.
    d. correct their written work.

True or False

Determine if each statement is true or false.

1. A linguistic series teaches word families (cat, hat, sat, pat, mat) rather than individual letter sounds.

    a. TRUE
    b. FALSE

2. Creating rhymes is an example of a phonemic awareness training activity.

    a. TRUE
    b. FALSE

3. The SPACE strategy is intended to help students figure out unfamiliar words.

    a. TRUE
    b. FALSE

4. Teaching prefixes, suffixes and Latin roots to students are all included in structural analysis.

    a. TRUE
    b. FALSE

5. During reciprocal teaching, students assume the role of teacher.

    a. TRUE
    b. FALSE

6. Repeated readings promote reading fluency in students with reading difficulties.

    a. TRUE
    b. FALSE

7. Cover-Copy-Compare is a strategy for studying spelling words.

    a. TRUE
    b. FALSE

Short Answer/Essay

1. Jerry is a student in your 4th grade general education class who has a learning disability. He is good at math but cannot read well. He thinks stories are dumb and would much rather play on the computer. He is not able to sound out written words he does not know or show interest in memorizing sight words. But he likes to tell stories to the other children about TV shows he watches such as DragonBall Z. He is somewhat disruptive during reading time since he is off task.

    a. What are the strengths and needs of the student?
    b. What are 3 possible modifications or interventions you could use to help Jerry to be successful with reading?

2. Why is fluency important for reading? Adults usually are not asked to read aloud in most situations. Why are children asked to read aloud?

3. Students with writing disabilities can now use word processing software on a computer. What are the benefits of using a word processing program on a computer? What are the problems of relying solely on computers for writing? What skills do students need to learn in order to use word processing programs?

4. What are some ways to test students on spelling words they use in their writing? How can you encourage students to attempt words they do not spell well? What are 3 ways to improve your students' spelling?

5. A new medical research study found evidence that students with dyslexia (reading disabilities) may have limited ability to hear sounds that rhyme. If their reading difficulties stem from an auditory perception problem, what would be some other ways to teach reading that do not require decoding? What methods would increase their skills with word attack and decoding?

For more activities related to chapter content, go to the Activities module in Chapter 13 of the Companion Website at www.prenhall.com/mastropieri.

Chapter 14: Mathematics

Objectives

After studying this chapter, you should be able to:

- Describe, evaluate, and implement various mathematical strategies from early number concepts to more advanced computations such as quadratic equations.
- Provide instructional strategies for such concepts as counting, one-to-one correspondence, numeration, Geometry, number lines, writing numbers, and understanding symbols.
- Describe and implement strategies for remembering addition and subtraction facts.
- List early addition and subtraction problem-solving strategies and multiplication and division concepts such as count-bys and count-ons, and describe how they can be implemented with students with special needs.
- Identify teaching strategies for incorporating calculators and introducing new vocabulary for multiplication and division facts, and describe when these strategies are appropriate.
- Understand and implement multiplication and division algorithm strategies such as priority of operations, Demonstration Plus Permanent Model, and modeling of long division.
- Describe and implement strategies in mathematics for operations on money, time, and fractions.
- Explain the use of manipulative materials and strategies for computation, solving quadratic equations, and problem solving in algebra.
- Describe and evaluate strategies for mathematical reasoning, such as graduated coaching, providing support for inventing concepts and procedures, and teaching functional math.

Chapter Outline

I. MATHEMATICS EDUCATION
II. MATHEMATICS AND STUDENTS WITH DISABILITIES
III. STRATEGIES FOR TEACHING MATH IN INCLUSIVE SETTINGS
    A. Early Number Concepts
    B. Teaching Students to Count
    C. One-to-One Correspondence
    D. Helping Students Master Numeration
    E. Introducing Geometry in Early Years
    F. Addition and Subtraction Concepts
    G. Counting with Number Lines
    H. Writing Numbers
    I. Understanding Symbols
    J. Addition and Subtraction Computation
        1. Touch Math
    K. Remembering Addition and Subtraction Facts
        1. Bley and Thornton's addition strategies
        2. Subtraction facts
    L. Place Value and Regrouping
    M. Teaching Early Problem Solving with Addition and Subtraction
    N. Multiplication and Division Concepts
        1. Count-bys
    O. Multiplication and Division Facts

P.   Calculators
Q.   Arithmetic Vocabulary
R.   Multiplication and Division Algorithms
       1.   Priority of operations
       2.   Demonstration plus permanent model
       3.   Modified long division
S.   Error Analysis for Diagnosis
T.   Problem Solving
       1.   Use of word meanings
       2.   Cognitive strategies
U.   Metacognition and Mathematics
V.   Money
W.   Time
X.   Fractions
Y.   Decimals
Z.   Area and Volume Concepts
       1.   Provide visual representations
       2.   Teach "big ideas"
AA.   Algebra
       1.   Use manipulatives to teach negative numbers
       2.   Teach algebraic representations early
       3.   Teach computation strategies
       4.   Teach strategies for solving quadratic equations
       5.   Teach problem-solving strategies
BB.   Mathematical Reasoning Problems
       1.   Use graduated coaching
       2.   Provide support for inventing concepts and procedures
CC.   Teach functional math

IV.   SUMMARY

Chapter Overview

- Mathematics has been considered the "key to opportunity" in society. However, many students with disabilities and other special needs exhibit problems learning mathematics. Appropriate curriculum, effective teaching, and specific strategy instruction can help alleviate many of these problems.

- Basic number and operation concepts (e.g., addition, subtraction) can be enforced by direct teaching, number lines, and manipulatives such as base 10 blocks. Learning of vocabulary concepts can be promoted by direct teaching, manipulatives, and verbal elaboration including mnemonic strategies.

- Learning of basic math facts can become a significant obstacle to many students with disabilities and other special needs. When possible, promote memory of basic facts through direct teaching, increased learning time, peer tutoring, specialized software, and independent study strategies. Additionally, use specific strategies for promoting recall of specific facts. If basic fact learning seems unproductive and frustrating, consider using calculators to continue progressing on other areas of mathematics functioning. Return to fact learning when it appears it may be profitable.

- Math word problem solving can be facilitated by using a concrete to semiconcrete to abstract sequence of instruction. In addition, use specific problem-solving strategies including a seven-step self-monitoring strategy, judicious use of clue words, highlighting, imagery, pictures, and other problem-solving strategies.

- Important money and time concepts can be enforced by direct teaching, increased practice, manipulatives, models, and providing a careful sequence of skills.
- Specific manipulative materials (commercially available or teacher-made) can be helpful in promoting learning of fractions and decimals. Specific self-monitoring and other strategies can also be useful in promoting these concepts.
- Promote concepts in algebra by providing early concept development, computation strategies, manipulatives such as algebra tiles, mnemonics, and self-monitoring strategies.
- Provide sufficient guidance and support when employing "invention" or "discovery" strategies. If students exhibit difficulty, break conceptual tasks into smaller units and allow students to use their reasoning skills on these subskills.
- Ensure that students are acquiring sufficient "practical" mathematics skills for use in transition to community life and future employment. Curriculum materials are available that provide for instruction in these practical areas.

Multiple Choice

Select the statement that best answers each multiple choice question.

1. _____ is the concept that sets of different objects (beads, blocks, etc.) can be matched with respect to quantity.

    a. Attribution training
    b. One-to-one correspondence
    c. Factual learning
    d. Touch Math

2. Students with difficulty writing numbers may benefit from the use of:

    a. Number concept development
    b. Visual discrimination activities
    c. Dashed-line numbers
    d. All of the above

3. In Touch Math, numbers higher than 5 are represented with

    a. squares.
    b. double touch points.
    c. colored highlighting.
    d. pegwords.

4. Placing quotation marks around a quotient is an example of

    a. concept enhancement.
    b. manipulative strategy.
    c. verbal elaboration.
    d. graduated coaching.

5. Miller and Mercer (1993b) demonstrated a word problem solving sequence strategy that included which levels of instruction?

   a. Concrete
   b. Semiconcrete
   c. Abstract
   d. All of the above

6. A strategy for helping students determine the priority of operations in an equation is

   a. FOIL.
   b. clue word.
   c. My Dear Aunt Sally.
   d. pegword strategy.

7. A bridge between multiplication concepts and facts is the use of

   a. count-bys.
   b. base 10 blocks.
   c. new doubles.
   d. doubles-plus-one.

8. The "ask for one, tell for one" strategy is intended to help students

   a. determine decimal equivalents.
   b. determine implied operations.
   c. read the hands of a clock.
   d. use regrouping procedures.

9. Which strategy or materials are intended to enhance the concept of equivalence in fractions?

   a. Fraction Burgers
   b. "Yodai" mnemonics
   c. Pattern Blocks
   d. All of the above

10. Which is intended to enhance the understanding of negative numbers?

   a. Quadratic equations
   b. Self-monitoring sheets
   c. Algebra tiles
   d. All of the above

True or False

Determine if each statement is true or false.

1. Counting is important but is not a necessary prerequisite skill to addition or subtraction.
   a. TRUE
   b. FALSE

2. "Count-ons" and "pattern nine facts" are strategies to assist students with division and multiplication facts.

   a. TRUE
   b. FALSE

3. An advantage of modified long division is that it allows students to view the entire problem.

   a. TRUE
   b. FALSE

4. Demonstration plus permanent model means that the teacher demonstrates the problem then the student models it back.
   a. TRUE
   b. FALSE

5. Numbers in number lines can go in either direction, with higher number to the left or right. It depends on the preference of the student.
   a. TRUE
   b. FALSE

6. That volume formulas represent the area of the base times a multiple of the height is an example of a "big idea."
   a. TRUE
   b. FALSE

7. Self-monitoring sheets are known to be useful for students struggling with math problem solving.
   a. TRUE
   b. FALSE

Short Answer/Essay

1. Jake has TBI and cannot use his arms or legs well. His speech is understandable but is very slow and laborious. Jake tires easily and cannot last the whole day at your middle school. So he takes your math class during second period. Jake gets around on a motorized wheelchair but has no educational assistance. Today you are teaching algebraic equations and the students are writing answers on the board. How do you include Jake? How do you check his understanding?

   a. What are the strengths and needs of the student?
   b. What are 3 possible modifications or interventions you could use to help Jake to be successful with his math class work?

2. Is counting on one's fingers an acceptable practice for mathematics? What would be your rationale for encouraging or discouraging this practice among your students?

3. Teachers are encouraged to use manipulative materials to teach mathematic concepts. What would be appropriate manipulative materials to use with younger students that would be inexpensive? How about for older students?

4. The researchers say to teach word problems with concrete, semi-concrete and abstract concepts. Give an example of each for teaching a multiplication word problem to students in an elementary classroom.

For more activities related to chapter content, go to the Activities module in chapter 14 of the Companion Website at www.prenhall.com/mastropieri.

Activities

1. Many gifted students are taught in general education classes. What are strategies you would use to teach gifted students in your mathematics class? Though the article below gives many good suggestions, which do you believe would be the most practical for a primary school teacher? Or a secondary school teacher?

Teaching Mathematics to Gifted Students in a Mixed-Ability Classroom
http://www.kidsource.com/education/teach.gift.math.html

2. View the video clip at the first web page below. You may need to download Quicktime (http://www.apple.com/quicktime/download/) to view it. It features Kent who is a student with a cognitive disability -- moderate mental retardation. In this clip you see him participating in a math activity involving space shapes with peers who are modeling for him.

Whole Schooling Consortium-Kent Learning Math with Peers Video Clip
http://www.coe.wayne.edu/wholeschooling/WS/Video/Mathlesson.html

Whole Schooling Consortium
http://www.coe.wayne.edu/CommunityBuilding/WSC.html

3. Illuminations, sponsored by the NCTM, has the best repository of math lessons on the web. One excellent tool is their collection of mathematics teaching video clips that encourage teacher reflection (found at the second webpage below). The first web page below contains a video clip of students working together to figure out fractional amounts of some manipulative materials. See the first video clip and answer the discussion questions below it.

NCTM Illuminations: Inquiry on Practice - Gathering Evidence
http://illuminations.nctm.org/reflections/3-5/GatheringEvidence/index.html

NCTM Illuminations: Inquiry on Practice
http://illuminations.nctm.org/reflections/

4. Manipulative materials are very useful for teaching mathematical concepts to students. If you are not fortunate enough to be given enough manipulative materials for your classroom try the following options. The first two web sites let you use virtual manipulative materials to teach your class. They can also be used in conjunction with manipulative materials. The third website provides templates that you can print on cardstock to create you own handmade math manipulative materials. What would be the advantages and disadvantages of using virtual manipulatives over concrete materials?

NCTM Illuminations: I-Math Investigations
http://illuminations.nctm.org/imath/index.html

Utah State University: The National Library of Virtual Manipulatives for Interactive Mathematics
http://matti.usu.edu/nlvm/nav/vlibrary.html

Hand Made Manipulative Instructions by Margo L. Mankus
http://mason.gmu.edu/~mmankus/Handson/manipulatives.htm

5. Algorithms are the procedures a person takes to solve a mathematics problem. We all were taught ways to do addition, subtraction, multiplication and division, but they were not necessarily the best or easiest way to learn these procedures. Try out the following example to see if it may be easier for addition if a student is easily distracted or has poor memory. For more information on alternative algorithms see more examples at the web pages at the end of this activity.

Low-Stress Addition: 292 + 875 + 439 + 678=

```
            2  2  2
               2  9  2
               4 11
               8  7  5
              12  8  7
               4  3  9
               6 11 16
    +          6  7  8
              12  8 14
         2  2  8  4
```

The Many Ways of Arithmetic in UCSMP Everyday Mathematics by Bas Braams
http://www.math.nyu.edu/mfdd/braams/links/em-arith.html

EveryDay Mathematics FAQ's
http://everydaymath.uchicago.edu/parents/faqs.shtml#3

Chapter 15: Science and Social Studies

Objectives

After studying this chapter, you should be able to:

- Describe and apply strategies for adapting textbook/content-oriented approaches in science and social studies such as content enhancements, semantic feature analysis, and mnemonic strategies.
- Identify criteria for selecting and adopting textbooks for your class or school district.
- Evaluate and implement strategy instruction for using content area textbooks such as text organization, text structure, and essential information in content textbooks.
- Describe and evaluate methods for adapting textbook materials to accommodate diverse learners in the classroom.
- Discuss considerations and adaptations to science activities and ways to make appropriate adaptations for teaching process skills.
- Provide methods and strategies for adapting activities in specific science content areas, including life science, earth science, and physical science activities for diverse learners.
- Describe and apply methods for adapting social studies with students with special needs.
- Discuss ways for adapting inquiry-oriented approaches in science and social studies.

Chapter Outline

I. SCIENCE AND SOCIAL STUDIES EDUCATION
   A. Adapting Textbook/Content-Oriented Approaches
   B. Effective Teacher Presentations
      1. Content enhancements
      2. Semantic feature analysis
      3. POSSE
      4. Use mnemonic strategies
      5. Modify worksheet activities
   C. Promoting Independent Learning from Textbooks
      1. Criteria for selecting considerate textbooks
      2. Strategy instruction for using content area textbooks
         a. Familiarize students with text organization
         b. The use of text structures
         c. Show how to identify essential information in content texts
         d. Teach outlining
         e. Introduce study guides
      3. Teach learning strategies
         a. MultiPass
         b. IT FITS
         c. TRAVEL
   D. Adapting Textbook Materials to Accommodate Diverse Learners
      1. Steps to take before students start to read
      2. Steps to take after textbook reading activities
      3. Adaptations for students with visual impairments or severe reading problems
      4. Use classwide peer tutor

II. ADAPTING ACTIVITIES-ORIENTED APPROACHES IN SCIENCE AND SOCIAL STUDIES
    A. Adapting Science Activities
        1. Develop general laboratory procedures
            a. List rules
            b. Ensure safety
            c. Give clear directions
            d. Enhance stimulus value
            e. Prepare for spills
            f. Make adaptations for teaching process skills
            g. Monitor progress
        2. Life science activities
            a. Using microscopes
            b. Health considerations
        3. Earth science activities
        4. Physical science activities
    B. Social Studies Adaptations
        1. General recommendations
        2. Field trips
III. INQUIRY LEARNING IN SCIENCE AND SOCIAL STUDIES
    A. Use a Problem-Solving Model for Social Studies Instruction
    B. Promoting Active Thinking with Guided Questioning
    C. Developmental Considerations
    D. Develop Students' Abilities to Use Deductive Reasoning
IV. SUMMARY

Chapter Overview

- Much learning in science and social studies takes place in the context of textbook learning. To address the needs of diverse classrooms, teachers should evaluate their texts for "considerateness."
- Content enhancement devices are means for increasing recall and comprehension of content information, and include use of graphic organizers, study guides, diagrams, visual spatial displays, and mnemonics.
- Familiarization with text organization and structure can help students understand text content. Students can be taught to incorporate analysis of text structure into their study strategies. Highlighting, outlining, and study guides are also helpful.
- Textbooks can be adapted for students with reading problems with such methods as audiotaped texts, Braille or enlarged-print versions, simplified texts, or modified presentations.
- Before assigned readings, students can be prefamiliarized with new vocabulary and provided with advance organizers such as visual spatial displays, timelines, or concept maps.
- After assigned readings, students can be provided with reviews and summaries of the readings, practice with peers, and extra help sessions.
- Activities-oriented instruction can be helpful for students who have reading problems, or who benefit from the enhanced concreteness and meaningfulness afforded by such instruction.
- A variety of adaptations are available for accommodating special needs in such science activity areas as balancing and weighing, activities with plants and animals, anatomy, microscope activities, weather, rocks and minerals, and activities involving sound and light. These adaptations address specific need areas, and also can serve to enhance comprehension of the associated concepts.

- Adaptations can also be incorporated into social studies areas, including role-play, simulation activities, and field trips.
- Inquiry-oriented approaches to science and social studies, found in both textbook and activities approaches, can also be adapted for students with special needs. These adaptations include use of hands-on materials, carefully structured questioning, redirecting attention, and reinforcing divergent, independent thinking.

Multiple Choice

Select the statement that best answers each multiple choice question.

1. In a _____ approach, students undertake specific projects or experiments to enhance understanding of the subject.

   a. textbook-oriented
   b. activities-oriented
   c. content-oriented
   d. all of the above

2. Which of the following are examples of content enhancements?

   a. Graphic organizers
   b. Study guides
   c. Mnemonics
   d. All of the above

3. The O in the acronym POSSE stands for:

   a. Overview of chapter content
   b. Organizing predictions based upon the forthcoming text structure
   c. Opening discussion of main ideas within the text
   d. Operating on the structure of the text

4. Modified worksheets assist students with special needs by:

   a. Covering fewer concepts
   b. Enabling students to keep up with the pace of instruction
   c. Providing a different type of practice on lesson concepts
   d. All of the above

5. IT FITS is a strategy to help students:

   a. Outline chapter content
   b. Create visual displays
   c. Create mnemonic strategies
   d. Activate prior knowledge

6. Which of the following is a distinct type of text structure?

   a. Expository
   b. Cause-effect
   c. Narrative
   d. All of the above

7. After textbook reading activities, to promote mastery of content by all students:

   a. Review and highlight major points
   b. Pair students to summarize key points as partners
   c. Write summaries in visual spatial or graphical formats
   d. All of the above

8. Adaptations for activities involving magnetism and electricity include:

   a. Increase teacher lecture allocations
   b. Assign additional reading
   c. Connect a light bulb to flash when constructing telegraphs
   d. All of the above

9. Adaptations for activities involving the "physics of sound" include:

   a. Amplification of target sounds and reducing others
   b. Use rubber bands on waterphones
   c. Place tuning forks in water
   d. All of the above

10. Strategies for adapting inquiry-oriented approaches in science and social studies include:

    a. Direct instruction in basic content
    b. Assign peers to re-read text passages
    c. Use guided questioning
    d. All of the above

True or False

Determine if each statement is true or false.

1. Students with disabilities and other special needs rarely encounter difficulties with science and social studies textbooks.

   a. TRUE
   b. FALSE

2. Framed outlines refer to outlines students create within "frames" or units of content.

   a. TRUE
   b. FALSE

3. Students familiarize themselves with the organization of the chapter during the "size up" pass in the MultiPass strategy.

   a. TRUE
   b. FALSE

4. Though research supports the use of study guides, in science and social studies study guides will often confuse students with disabilities.

   a. TRUE
   b. FALSE

5. One modification a teacher may make on a worksheet is to enlarge the font for a student with visual impairments.

   a. TRUE
   b. FALSE

6. The TRAVEL strategy is designed to help students create their own cognitive organizers.

   a. TRUE
   b. FALSE

7. In some cases, deductive thinking activities may be a positive alternative to inductive inquiry methods.

   a. TRUE
   b. FALSE

Short Answer/Essay

1. Jade is a visually impaired student in your fifth grade general education class. She is articulate and bright, but hates to be singled out more than necessary. Although she can see when things are enlarged and held close to her face (she wears very thick glasses), she could not see your demonstration during today's science lesson when you demonstrated how to make a cloud in a jar (you are teaching about precipitation). Tomorrow you want the students to duplicate the experiment and write up their findings.

   a. What are the strengths and needs of the student?
   b. What are 3 possible modifications or interventions you could use to help this student be successful for her science experiment?

2. In many middle school and high school science classes, the students are assigned lab partners for science experiments. What characteristics would you look for in a student that you may pair up with a student with disabilities? Would you keep permanent lab partners or change them? How would a lab partner be able to assist a student with disabilities?

3. A common modification for a student with lower reading skills is to give them materials from publishers that have science and social studies content, but written at a lowered reading level. Adolescents are very concerned about being perceived as different from their peers. How do you assign work to the student in this alternate book for homework without making it clear to everyone in the class?

For more activities related to chapter content, go to the Activities module in chapter 15 of the Companion Website at www.prenhall.com/mastropieri.

Chapter 16: Art, Music, Physical Education, Foreign Languages, Vocational Education, and Transitions

Objectives

After studying this chapter, you should be able to:

- Describe and implement adaptations for students with special needs in art, music, physical education, foreign languages, and vocational and career education.
- Understand the importance of setting realistic vocational and career goals and objectives as well as environmental, curriculum, and instructional strategies and modifications.
- Identify the meaning of transition and the purpose of planning and designing transition programs for students with disabilities.
- Gain an understanding of the significance of teaching self-advocacy and self-determination skills toward promoting assertiveness and advocacy.
- Understand the importance of planning and transitioning for graduation, future education, job opportunities, and independent living.

Chapter Outline

I. ART, MUSIC, PHYSICAL EDUCATION
    A.   Teaching Strategies
    B.   Foreign Languages

II. VOCATIONAL AND CAREER EDUCATION
    A.   Overview of Vocational and Career Education
    B.   The Carl D. Perkins Vocational Education Act of 1984
    C.   Modifications for Students with Special Needs
        1.   Goals and objectives
        2.   Environmental modifications
        3.   Curriculum modifications
            a.   Plan for safety considerations
            b.   Modify instructional materials
            c.   Select computer software
        4.   Instructional strategies
            a.   Teach procedures
            b.   Increase time on task
            c.   Individualize instruction
    D.   Generalizable Skills

III. TRANSITIONS
    A.   What Does Transition Mean?
        1.   Make preparations with students to plan for transitions
        2.   Plan transitions to adulthood
    B.   Self-Advocacy and Self-Determination Preparation
        1.   Teach strategies
        2.   Learning assertiveness
    C.   Assessment
    D.   Curriculum
    E.   Planning for Graduation

      F.   Planning for Future Education
      G.   Planning for Future Job Opportunities
      H.   Planning for Independent Living Situations
IV.   SUMMARY

Chapter Overview

- Art, music, and physical education are important subject areas for students with disabilities. Prioritize objectives and adapt the environment, instructional materials, and procedures effectively in art, music, and physical education to ensure success for students with disabilities.
- Foreign languages may be particularly challenging subjects for students with disabilities, and extra care should be taken to ensure that sufficient modifications are in place to assist students with appropriate modifications.
- Vocational education and career education include a wide variety of educational programs that are intended to prepare students for employment and for living. Vocational education may be particularly important for students with disabilities or other special needs who become employed immediately after high school.
- Vocational education areas include agriculture, business, family and consumer sciences, marketing, health, trade and industry, and technical/communications.
- The Carl D. Perkins Vocational Act of 1984 was of significant importance in promoting access to vocational education for students with disabilities or other special needs.
- Special considerations for adapting instruction to students with special needs include modifying the physical environment, choosing goals and objectives carefully, adapting curriculum materials, and adapting instructional procedures.
- Transitions in life are important, and transition planning is critical for students with disabilities. All students with IEPs must have Individual Transition Plans by the age of 14 or the end of eighth grade.
- Prepare students of all ages for transitions, including transitions from home to preschool, to new schools, to new teachers, and most importantly, for life after high school. Involve students, parents, teachers, counselors, transition coordinators, and community-based personnel as members of the transition team.
- Students with disabilities require instruction in self-advocacy and self-determination skills to provide them with skills to be more successful during and after high school. Provide ample practice in safe environments for the development of these skills.
- Prepare students for life after high school by using appropriate transition assessment measures, carefully evaluating the results, and designing and implementing life skills programs.
- Help prepare students for the appropriate high school graduation requirements necessary for their transition plans.
- Provide educational opportunities that prepare students with disabilities for future education, jobs, and independent or supported living arrangements.

Multiple Choice

Select the statement that best answers each multiple choice question.

1. Individuals with disabilities have exhibited outstanding achievement in:

    a. Art
    b. Music
    c. Athletics
    d. All of the above

2. Some adaptations for students with special needs in physical education do NOT include:

    a. Have students with disabilities play in another gym
    b. Modify the way students are placed on competitive teams
    c. Prioritize objectives and modifications to game rules
    d. Substitute standard equipment for more easily handled equipment

3. Instructional methods used in foreign language classes rely upon good:

    a. Listening skills
    b. Phonemic awareness
    c. Auditory discrimination
    d. All of the above

4. One helpful way to address safety considerations is

    a. developing a "safety profile."
    b. frequent testing.
    c. lecturing on safety.
    d. increasing readings.

5. _____ requires that vocational education for students with disabilities be delivered in the least-restrictive environment.

    a. The Elementary and Secondary Education Act
    b. The Perkins Act
    c. The Americans with Disabilities Act
    d. None of the above

6. Which of the following are modifications to the curriculum to initiate vocational and career education?

    a. Prioritize objectives
    b. Adapt environment, curriculum, and instruction
    c. Systematically evaluate progress toward meeting objectives
    d. All of the above

7. In vocational programs, goals and objectives should be

   a. realistic.
   b. the same as other students.
   c. competitive.
   d. high and ambitious.

8. The three types of activities specified in individualizing instruction in vocational areas include:

   a. Written assignments
   b. Audio-visual presentations
   c. Laboratory assignments
   d. All of the above

9. The first step in the I PLAN strategy is to

   a. develop a list of relevant questions.
   b. develop a self-inventory of strengths and needs.
   c. identify goals for the future.
   d. isolate procedures to help you accomplish your goals.

10. After students with disabilities leave high school, they have rights under:

   a. Americans with Disabilities Act
   b. IDEA
   c. Their IEPs
   d. All of the above

True or False

Determine if each statement is true or false.

1. Learning disabilities prevent individuals from high achievement in art, music, or athletics.

   a. TRUE
   b. FALSE

2. Musical books and scores are cannot be printed in large print or Braille.

   a. TRUE
   b. FALSE

3. Self-advocacy should only be taught to students with mild disabilities.

   a. TRUE
   b. FALSE

4. Business education, marketing education, and health occupations education are all areas of vocational education.

    a. TRUE
    b. FALSE

5. The purpose of a technical terms tabulation sheet is to document when a particular term will be discussed.

    a. TRUE
    b. FALSE

6. Generalizable skills include a set of teaching strategies to promote generalization.

    a. TRUE
    b. FALSE

7. There are several organizations that assist persons with disabilities with a variety of athletic activities.

    a. TRUE
    b. FALSE

Short Answer/Essay

1. Jordan is now 14 years old and is getting ready for his first transition planning meeting. Jordan has spina bifida, uses a wheelchair, and has to use a shunt to control the build-up of cerebral-spinal fluid on his brain. He has mild hydrocepaphy, which caused some brain damage. He loves art and has shown some real talent with his cartoons. He says he wants to grow up to be an artist, but you are not sure if it is realistic since his academic skills are quite low. But you do not want to dash his dreams and tell him he should consider other plans until you know more about his options. What can you do to prepare him and yourself for this transition meeting?

    a. What are the strengths and needs of the student?
    b. What additional information would be helpful to have?
    c. How can you assist Jordan in reaching or changing his goals?

2. If a student has significant delays in reading should she be excluded from art, physical education, and/or music so that she can have additional time for reading instruction or practice? Please give specific reasons for your answer.

3. An Individual Transition Plan (ITP) also concerns itself with the student learning daily living skills and having leisure interests. Is it the schools' responsibility to provide these skills or interests to their students? Why are these important? When are they provided to students that do not have disabilities?

4. Finding employment is a large undertaking for everyone. What are some of the skills all students, not just ones with disabilities, need in order to find and get a job?

For more activities related to chapter content, go to the Activities module in chapter 16 of the Companion Website at www.prenhall.com/mastropieri.

Chapter 1: Introduction to Inclusive Teaching Answer Key

Multiple Choice

1. Which is NOT one of the disability categories included and served under Individuals with Disabilities Education Act (IDEA)?

    b. Students at risk for school failure

2. Which of the following is one of the principles of The Individuals with Disabilities Education Act (IDEA)?

    b. For students with disabilities to receive a free and appropriate education

3. What term means, "students with disabilities must be educated in a setting least removed from the general education classroom?"

    c. Least-Restrictive Environment

4. Which of the following educational placements represent an example from the "Continuum of Services"?

    c. General education classroom with resource room services

5. Which of the following is NOT a related service provided under IDEA to assist students with disabilities?

    b. Reduced insurance/medical rates

6. In a _____ model of instruction, students with specialized needs receive all or most of their major instruction from special education teachers.

    a. self-contained

7. In the 1980s, what movement was initiated to provide a model for educating students with disabilities—particularly those students with mild and moderate disabilities—totally within the general education environment?

    b. Regular Education Initiative

8. Which of the following benefits is NOT usually predicted for the full-inclusion model?

    d. Professional Development

True or False

1. The Individuals with Disabilities Education Act (IDEA) is a federal law stating ALL students are entitled to a "free and appropriate education."

TRUE

2. Today, nearly seventy-five percent of students with disabilities are served primarily in general education classrooms.

TRUE

3. Section 504 (of the Vocational Rehabilitation Act) is a law preventing discrimination of students with disabilities in all federally funded institutions and workplaces.

TRUE

4. Least Restrictive Environment means to teach students with disabilities in the general education classroom.

FALSE

5. The individualized family service plan (IFSP) replaces the individualized education plan (IEP) when other family members also need special services.

FALSE

6. Many proponents of full inclusion believe that full-time placement in the general education classroom is a basic right of all students, including students with disabilities.

TRUE

7. Teachers are given the choice of whether or not to include students with disabilities in their classes.

FALSE

Short Answer/Essay

1. What are the major differences between historical and current practices toward individuals with disabilities?

Historically, services were not provided to individuals with special needs. Current practices include a variety of services and the law mandates schooling for individuals with disabilities.

2. How do the 6 principles of IDEA protect the rights of students and parents? Give an example for each principle.

1) Zero reject
2) Nondiscriminatory testing
3) Free and appropriate education
4) Least restrictive environment
5) Due Process
6) Parent participation

Examples may vary

3. Give examples of how a student with disabilities may be stigmatized by (1) pulling him or her out of the classroom to receive special education services and (2) providing him or her special education services in the general education classroom.

In a pull-out class the child may feel embarrassment at having to leave the room for services, but in an inclusive setting he or she may also be embarrassed if a teacher has to work with him or her individually. Examples may vary.

4. What does the expression "special education is a service, not a place" mean when discussing the continuum of services?

Examples may vary. One point may be that special education used to be exclusively a pull-out system, whereas now there are many services provided in the general education setting. Another point may be that special education children are still the responsibility of general education, and just receive special education services. They do not "belong to special education" which implies that the responsibility belongs solely to the special education teacher. The responsibility is shared.

5. What laws or portions of a law are the following scenarios violating?
- Jose is tested for special education after his Non-English speaking parents initial a consent form in English. (IDEA)
- Jamal is given an IQ in English even though he speaks only Arabic. (IDEA)
- Julie is told she cannot work as a paraprofessional since she has mild cerebral palsy and uses a walker. (ADA)
- Jacqueline, who has muscular dystrophy, is told that she cannot attend her neighborhood school since they do not have accessibility ramps for her wheelchair. (Section 504)
- The school district changed the number of hours Jeremy is receiving special education services and then informed the parents without holding an IEP meeting. (IDEA)

Chapter 2: Collaboration: Partnerships and Procedures Answer Key

Multiple Choice

1. Which is NOT a component of effective communication?

    d. Constructive criticism

2. Information often submitted with a formal prereferral intervention request includes:

    d. All of the above

3. Changing seating positions and rearranging desks are types of

    a. environmental modifications.

4. Which of the following is generally considered to be the most effective co-teaching model?

    d. None of the above

5. Services identified by the case conference committee as related services include:

    d. All of the above

6. Individualized Transition Plans (ITPs) are required to be written into student IEPs beginning at _____ years of age.

    c. 14

7. Short-term objectives included on an IEP do NOT include which of the following?

        c. Meeting annual goals

8. Re-evaluations of students with IEPs can be requested:

        c. At any time

9. Due process refers to

        c. how conflicts between parents and schools are resolved.

10. A _____ assists in mediating disputes and/or conflicts between parents and the school district regarding the student's education or disagreements on eligibility, outcomes of the educational evaluation, or other aspects of the IEP.

        a. mediator

True or False

1. The prereferral intervention process is a part of the special education IEP process.

FALSE

2. An individualized education program includes a statement explaining the extent to which a student may not be participating with children without disabilities.

TRUE

3. Transportation services are NOT relevant to a student's IEP.

FALSE

4. In the co-teaching strategy "alternative teaching," teachers teach similar content but may use different approaches depending on student needs.

TRUE

5. Mediation is a voluntary process that must be requested by both parties.

TRUE

6. Parents are clear on their roles in inclusive collaboration.

FALSE

7. Paraprofessionals are only responsible for non-educational tasks.

FALSE

Short Answer/Essay

1. What are the steps to effective communication? Give an example of a time you had to work on a project with others and went through each of the processes to collaboratively accomplish the task?

Examples may vary. The steps to effective communication include: active listening, depersonalize situations, find common goals, brainstorm possible solutions, summarize goals and solutions, and follow up to monitor progress.

2. Which of the following IEP objectives would be easier for you to follow as a teacher?
    A.   Johan will learn multiplication this year on grade level.
    B.   When given a teacher made test of 30 multiplication problems with single digits on a timed test, Johan will complete 25 out of 30 problems correctly in 5 minutes.

What would you do if you did not understand an IEP objective for a student of yours?

B is easier to follow since it is specific. I would ask the special education teacher to help clarify it, and/or members of the previous IEP team meeting.

3. You are told to co-teach with a special education teacher. You have always taught every subject to your elementary students and are a bit reluctant to let someone else take over your class. But you always felt you could do much more with another adult in the classroom. What co-teaching arrangement would you prefer? Is there a subject area you would be willing to let him or her be responsible for teaching your class? Or would you only be comfortable with him or her working in a supportive role? What benefits would there be if one of you were teaching while the other was monitoring how well the students understood the lesson?

Answers and examples may vary. Should choose one of the following: Station teaching, Parallel teaching, Alternative Teaching, Complementary Instruction, Supportive Learning Activities, or Team Teaching.

Chapter 3: Teaching Students with Higher-Incidence Disabilities Answer Key

Multiple Choice

1. Higher-incidence disability areas comprise approximately _____ of students served under IDEA.

    d. 90%

2. Classroom adaptations for students with speech or language impairments include:

    d. All of the above

3. Lisping is an example of a(n)

    b. articulation disorder.

4. The disability area most widely represented in general education classes is

    c. learning disabilities.

5. Which condition does the federal definition of learning disabilities NOT include?

    d. Mental retardation

6. Students with moderate mental retardation represent a range of functioning represented by IQ scores between about:

    a. 35 to 54.

7. _____ is an example of a genetic disorder also referred to as Trisomy 21.

    d. Down syndrome

8. Which statement is true of students with emotional disturbance?

    a. Boys outnumber girls 5 to 1

9. Which is a criterion under IDEA (1996) regarding emotional disturbance?

    d. All of the above

10. Which of the following disorders are associated with emotional disturbance?

    a. Selective mutism

True or False

1. Stuttering is a common articulation disorder.

FALSE

2. Semantics refers to the meanings of words used in language.

TRUE

3. While most students with learning disabilities have difficulty learning to read, students with learning disabilities rarely exhibit difficulties learning mathematics.

FALSE

4. Children with learning disabilities are usually not identified until they enter school.

TRUE

5. Fewer than half (about 45%) of students with mental retardation have mild or moderate disabilities.

FALSE

6. Social maladjustment such as juvenile delinquency is a component of the IDEA definition of emotional disturbance.

FALSE

7. Students with emotional disturbance may not exhibit aggressive behaviors.

TRUE

Short Answer/Essay

1. Jacqui is very shy and will not speak in public. She has a speech impairment (lisp) that makes her self-conscious in your third-grade class. She does have a few close friends she will whisper to, and she will also speak to you if no one is around. You have oral book reports due next week in class. You want to encourage Jacqui to speak since she is supposed to practice her speech therapy, but you do not want to put her in a stressful situation.

a. What are the strengths and needs of the student?
b. What are 3 possible modifications or interventions you could use to help Jacqui to be successful on her oral report?

a. Strengths: will speak to teacher individually, has friends. Needs: Oral report but shy and does not like to speak in public.
b. Possible answers: 1. Jacqui can give her oral report during recess to you or you and her friends. 2. Jacqui can tape record her report and you can listen to it when she is not there. 3. Reports can be given in groups and Jacqui will be with friends and have only a small speaking part.

2. There will usually be students with high-incidence disabilities in your classroom every year. Research studies have demonstrated that adaptations used for students with special needs work even better for students without disabilities. Choose 3 suggestions from this chapter that you believe will help all of your students to achieve.

Answers will vary. The suggestions will include adaptations to the physical environment, choosing goals and objectives carefully, adapting curriculum materials, and adapting instructional procedures.

3. Many students have organizational problems (so do many teachers!). What are some ways that you can organize your classroom at the beginning of the year to assist your students and you in organization?

Answers will vary. Answers may include having cubby holes or lockers for student belongings, students will use folders or have organizational notebooks structured for your class. You can also establish a place to turn in papers.

4. If a 14 year old student with mental retardation wanted to sit on your lap and hug you, would you think that action was appropriate? Why or why not? What would you say to the student?

Hugging and lap sitting is not appropriate at school, especially at 14 years old, and should be discouraged. This is the type of behavior that will make life difficult for students with mental retardation. They should be expected to act age appropriately as much as possible. They are not "children". Though you never want to be harsh and embarrass a student in front of others, you do need to be firm and say no while suggesting a more age appropriate behavior. The best response is, " I am glad you want to show me affection. I like you too. But in school it is best to show affection by giving me a big smile." Later you can have a discussion about appropriate and inappropriate touching in school.

Chapter 4: Teaching Students with Lower-Incidence Disabilities Answer Key

Multiple Choice

1. Individuals with _____ comprise one of the smallest disability areas, accounting for only about 0.5% of individuals with disabilities classified under IDEA.

    b. visual impairments

2. Potential causes of hearing impairments include:

    a. Maternal rubella

3. Orthopedic impairments involve damage to the:

    b. Skeletal system

4. Health conditions referred to as Other Health Impairments include:

    c. Allergies and asthma

5. _____ is a common neurological disorder that causes permanent disorders of movement and positions.

    a. Cerebral palsy

6. Commonly provided adaptations for students with traumatic brain injuries include:

    b. Providing a shortened school day

7. Which of the following is true of muscular dystrophy?

    d. Children should be lifted only by those with explicit training.

8. _____ is an inherited condition in which sugar is not metabolized correctly due to insufficient production of insulin in the pancreas.

    d. Diabetes

9. It is estimated that _____ of individuals with autism may never develop language.

    c. 50%

10. A common characteristic of autism is:

    b. Stereotypic behavior

True or False

1. Individuals are classified as legally blind if their visual acuity is less than 20/100 with corrective lenses.

TRUE

2. Retinitis pigmentosa is a common cause of hearing impairment.

FALSE

3. Cerebral palsy is progressive in nature, which means it worsens over time.

FALSE

4. In any seizure, do not place any object between the teeth of the affected person.

TRUE

5. Children with chronic illnesses should do most of their work in the afternoon after they have had a chance to warm-up in the morning.

FALSE

6. "Curriculum overlapping" is a technique for including students with severe and multiple disabilities into general education class curriculum and activities.

TRUE

7. Teachers should not ask about medications that a child might be taking since that violates the patient-doctor confidentiality.

FALSE

Short Answer/Essay

1. Jill has diabetes and has to watch her sugar intake. She participates in all of your elementary classes activities with no problems. But you like to reward the students with candy at times. Plus there are several parties planned for the year. You don't want to have to exclude Jill from the sweets but you also do not think it is fair to deprive your whole class either. You also do not want to have to make sure she is not eating something she should not. What can you do to make sure Jill is included but not singled out in front of the class?

> Answers will vary but the point is to have sensitivity towards Jill. You can have a reward jar with treats but make sure there are some toys, pencils, or stickers as options as well as candy so Jill can be rewarded too. Don't announce, "Jill make sure not to choose a candy!" Just let her choose what she wants, and she knows not to pick the treats. Ask if there are foods she likes that she can have during parties so that she can participate. Most children with diabetes monitor themselves well and do not need a lot of supervision for their eating (unless you are told otherwise), but they do need some understanding. Make sure not to make a big deal of her difference to the class and she will appreciate it.

2. Teachers who are new to teaching students with low-incidence disabilities may not know how to handle interactions with students with special needs. What would you do in the following situations?

- A student limps by your classroom on her way to lunch. You notice her since it is your planning time. She wears crutches since she has cerebral palsy. She also makes soft whimpering sounds when she passes by and looks at you with sad eyes. Since she does not weigh much you want to carry her to the cafeteria. What should you do or say? Why?

You may want to carry the student, but will you be available to do it the rest of her life? If not, fight the urge. She does not need your sympathy; she needs your encouragement. This is based on a real student who played this trick on every new teacher (who all fell for it). Experienced teachers understand that all children need to learn independence. To do more for your students sometimes handicaps them for when you are not there.

- You see some observers walking by a male high school student in a wheelchair who is in an aisle. As the women observers walk by, the student pats them on their posteriors. So far no one has said anything to the student. You are the next one who needs to walk by him. What should you do or say? Why?

You should let him know in no uncertain terms that touching you in any way would be met with strict disapproval. Since he has an obvious disability, the observers were not sure if he understood what he was doing. But you should know that even if he did not know (which is doubtful) he might as well learn now. Fondling strangers as they walk by is not socially acceptable by anyone! The longer this student believes it is acceptable, the harder it will be to break him of the habit. So he might as well learn it starting with you. Social skills are very important, and disregarding them out of sympathy is a disservice to the individual with a disability.

3. Classroom arrangement can be very important for students with certain types of disabilities. What are some classroom accommodations you would make for a student with a wheelchair? What are some classroom accommodations you would make for a student who is blind and uses a cane?

Some answers may vary. For a student in a wheelchair I would make the aisles wide around tables and desks. I would also seat him or her near the door. For a student who is blind I would also seat him near the door and make sure he knows where everything is in the class. I would try to make sure that things were not moved around without telling the student.

4. What plan of action would you have if a student of yours had a seizure? How would you be able to take care of your class and the student?

The main point is to have a plan ahead of time. Usually it involves making arrangements with another teacher to send your class to his or her room while you stay with the student with seizures. You should have a way to contact the school nurse and have the students' parents phone numbers readily available. Answers may vary somewhat.

Chapter 5: Teaching Students with Other Special Learning Needs Answer Key

Multiple Choice

1. Students with ADHD who do not meet the requirements for services under IDEA may qualify under

   b. Section 504 of the Vocational Rehabilitation Act.

2. The major cause of ADHD has been identified as:

   d. No single cause has been identified

3. According to the DSM-IV, which statement is false of ADHD?

   b. Symptomatic behaviors must persist for two years.

4. Many reports indicate that _____ of the population is gifted and talented.

   a. 3–5%

5. Which is NOT true of gifted, talented, or creative students?

   d. All of the above are true

6. Asian Americans have been found to be

   a. overrepresented in special education.

7. In the U.S. today, African Americans constitute:

   a. The largest minority group

8. _____ refers to having students from diverse cultural groups learn to "fit in" with the dominant cultural group and leave their own culture behind.

   b. Assimilation

9. Overrepresentation of some groups in special education may be due in part to:

     d. All of the above

10. Which of the following are resources for potential identification of students at risk?

     d. All of the above

True or False

1. Section 504 is an important part of the Individuals with Disabilities Education Act (IDEA).

FALSE

2. Research has identified food additives and sugar as the most likely causes of ADHD.

FALSE

3. Admitting a child to school early, or skipping grades, are some examples of acceleration programs.

TRUE

4. Cultural pluralism refers to fostering of differing cultural groups within the school setting.

TRUE

5. About half of homeless families are single mothers with an average of two to three children.

FALSE

6. Giving a gifted child independent work on a topic of his or her interest is an example of enrichment.

TRUE

7. Schools and teachers have the responsibility to report any signs of child abuse.

TRUE

Short Answer/Essay

1. Jimmy is a student in your 1st grade general education class who has ADHD. He has trouble paying attention for more than 5 minutes at a time and can't stay in his seat more than 10 minutes. Even when he is in his seat he is bouncing around and watching everyone and everything except you. You are tired of yelling at him to pay attention and to sit down. Though he apologizes each time, you know he will do it again. The other students are able to ignore his actions better than you do. But his actions are affecting his grades since he has trouble finishing assignments and tests. He is also behind in most subjects because he can't seem to focus on what is going on in class.

     a. What are the strengths and needs of this student?
     b. What are 3 possible modifications or interventions you could use to help Jimmy stay on task?

    a.   Strengths: Has a lot of energy; seems to mean well. Needs: Has to pay attention and stay on task.

b. Possible answers: Since Jimmy only attends for 5 minutes at a time, and is always out of his seat put that energy to work. 1. He can be the class pencil sharpener person, and pass out papers so he needs to be out of his seat for legitimate reasons. 2. Find an area in the back where he can do his work while standing at a counter or lying on a carpet and fidgeting. 3. Set a timer for every 5 minutes so he can self-monitor his attention and get himself back on task if he is off. You can pair it with a token reinforcement as well. There are many other solutions, but you need to know more about Jimmy and possibly try a few interventions out before you know which one will work.

2. Historically, many people from cultures that migrated to American wanted to learn English and be assimilated into the majority culture. More recently there has been an emphasis on cultural pluralism where immigrants retain a strong connection with their heritage. Assimilation has been described as a "melting pot" while Cultural Pluralism has been described more as a "salad bowl." What are the advantages and disadvantages of each practice? What are some ways you may integrate multicultural education into your classroom?

The advantage to assimilation is that a person learns to fit in with the majority and adopts their customs. The disadvantage of assimilation is the person may lose his or her own culture in the process. Cultural pluralism has the advantage of keeping one's culture, but it is sometimes difficult to do without spending time with people of the same culture. It takes effort to keep another culture when far from home. There are many ways to integrate multicultural education into the classroom including discussing different cultures, reading books, going to museums, exploring the arts, watching videos, eating different foods, and inviting speakers.

3. Is it appropriate to have your gifted students tutor your students who are having difficulties? When might this be appropriate? When is it not appropriate?

Answers may vary. Sometimes your gifted students love tutoring and they are good at it. In those cases, it may be appropriate to allow them to do some tutoring. But if you have a student who has real difficulty, then you may need to be the one instructing them. Plus, your gifted students should be doing work appropriate for their level. Just because a student is good at a skill does not mean they are good at teaching it to others, or are comfortable teaching their peers.

4. We tend to judge risk factors from our own experiences or from general information. But with individual students it is best to find out more information before jumping to conclusions. What else would you need to know before assuming that these students were at risk of dropping out of school? Who would you ask? Should you interfere or is it best to wait to see if the situation improves?
- Justin tells you his father left the family and that his parents are getting a divorce.
- June has been absent a lot due to illness.
- Jasmine is hanging out with a group of students you believe are taking drugs.
- Jamie comes to school in dirty clothes and has poor personal hygiene.

For each of these situations, it could be interpreted as a minor or major situation. Divorce may be a relief to Justin, and it was the marriage that was stressful. June may have a recurring ear infection that clears up after a few weeks. Jasmine may not be involved with drugs, even if her friends are involved. Jamie's washing machine may have temporarily broken. But they also could be much more serious. Justin's family may be homeless, June could have a major illness, Jasmine could be getting in trouble both physically and with the law, and Jamie may be neglected. Rather than assume, you need to ask the child or their parents as soon as you notice anything amiss. All of these signs if serious can lead to the student's failure at school. It is not interfering to find out what is going on with your students and try to find assistance when possible. It is your job.

Chapter 6: Effective Instruction for All Students Answer Key

Multiple Choice

1. Which is an important "effective teaching" variable?

   d. All of the above

2. The curriculum should:

   d. All of the above are true

3. Determining that one stimulus is either the same or different from another stimulus is

   b. discrimination learning.

4. Conceptual learning can be enhanced by:

   d. All of the above

5. The degree to which students are directly engaged physically and/or mentally in instruction is

   b. on-task behavior.

6. The SCREAM variables include all except:

   c. Consistency

7. Having all students choose or write down an answer before anyone responds is an example of

   b. covert responding.

8. Questioning generally should be fast-paced for:

   a. Basic skills and basic facts

9. The type of feedback delivered depends to some extent on

   c. the type of response that has been given.

10. In a model lesson, after daily review comes

   c. statement of purpose.

True or False

1. Monitoring the pace and instructional objectives are important considerations when planning content coverage.

TRUE

2. Remembering the steps in solving long division problems is an example of conceptual learning.

FALSE

3. A student transferring previously learned knowledge or skills to novel situations is known as generalization.

TRUE

4. Formative evaluation occurs at the end of a school year to determine how much was learned during the year.

FALSE

5. Identification criteria include pointing on a communication board, responding to matching, multiple-choice or true/false formats.

TRUE

6. An example of a streamlined transition activity is when students have assigned places to quickly line up in an orderly fashion to go to the cafeteria.

TRUE

7. Lower level questions are all that are appropriate for students with learning disabilities or mental retardation.

FALSE

Short Answer/Essay

1. Jana moved with her family last year to the United States from Germany. Her English is not that of a native speaker but she was taught English in Germany. Though she rarely speaks, when she does it is in a halting English. Jana is somewhat shy but she smiles a lot and has made one or two friends in your fifth grade class. She seems to understand well when you model activities or when you work with her individually. But whenever you teach the whole group she does not seem to understand or stay on-task. She does poorly on tests in all subjects. You are afraid she is at-risk for school failure.

    a.   What are the strengths and needs of the student?
    b.   What are 3 possible modifications or interventions you could use to help Jana to be successful in school?

    a.   Strengths: Some English, speaks German, has friends. Needs: poor comprehension in a group, off task, poor test scores
    b.   Possible answers: 1. Jana can work with a peer to help keep her on task since she does better with individual attention. 2. Learn a few German words to use with Jana when she seems to be not listening or off-task. 3. Talk to her parents and find out more about what kind of student she was in Germany and how Jana is adjusting to the move. They may have some good insights and suggestions. Brainstorm with them for some additional interventions.

2. What is wrong with the following objectives? A good objective includes content, conditions, and criteria. What could you add to each objective to improve it?

    a.   Jasper will read a 100-word passage out of a fifth-grade science book. (Missing criteria)
    b.   Jayleen will answer 4 out of 5 comprehension questions. (Missing conditions)
    c.   After reading 5 math word problems involving subtraction with regrouping, Justin will do them. (Missing content [behavior] and criteria)

3. Give an example for the SCREAM method. Explain what you would do for each of the following steps for a specific lesson.
- structure
- clarity
- redundancy
- enthusiasm
- appropriate rate
- maximized engagement

Answers will vary.

4. How can you maximize engagement through questioning? Give three examples of questions a teacher may ask about houses from around the world that would maximize student engagement.

Answers will vary. Some examples may be:
a. "Why do you think Japanese houses are smaller than houses we have in the United States?" This could lead to some brainstorming and a discussion about land amounts and space.
b. "Why were the houses in England made of stone while houses in Germany were mainly made of wood?" A discussion of resources could follow.
c. "Why are the windows of houses in the northern United States smaller than windows in Mexico?" A discussion about climate and weather can follow.

5. Identify the type of learning (discrimination, factual, rule, procedural, conceptual, or problem solving) for each of the following examples:
- Writing an essay on the causes of the economic highs and lows (Problem Solving)
- Telling the numbers "6" and "9" apart (Discrimination)
- Being able to identify an amphibian (Conceptual)
- Learning names of types of rocks (Factual)
- Learning how to add on a number line (Procedural)
- Learning to ask permission before getting out of seat (Rule)

Chapter 7: Improving Classroom Behavior and Social Skills Answer Key

Multiple Choice

1. One example of a "mistaken goal" (Dreikurs & Cassel, 1992) is

   a. concealing inadequacy.

2. Operationalized behaviors create behavioral objectives specifying:

   c. The criteria for acceptable performance

3. An "A-B-C" chart refers to:

   b. Antecedent, Behavior, Consequence.

4. When the observer tallies the number of times a particular behavior occurs, this is an example of

   a. event recording.

5. The first and most important step in classroom management is

        c. establishing and maintaining a positive, supportive classroom atmosphere.

6. _____ is a simple strategy of moving closer to students who are beginning to demonstrate inappropriate behavior.

        b. Proximity

7. Separation of the student from the routine classroom environment, usually for a violation of classroom rules, is referred to as

        c. timeout.

8. Which is NOT a characteristic of a level system?

        d. All of the above are true

9. The Good Behavior Game

        c. rewards groups or teams of students for good behavior.

10. Which is NOT an advantage of school-wide discipline system?

        d. The same rules are enforced in the same way throughout the school system

True or False

1. "Marco will exhibit on-task behavior in math class 85% of the time for four out of five consecutive days" is an operationalized behavior.

TRUE

2. Tangible reinforcers include snacks, drinks, and praise.

FALSE

3. Debriefing procedures typically occur after a specified period of timeout.

TRUE

4. The most important thing to remember in handling a confrontation is to remain calm.

TRUE

5. A student contract describes the rewards for exhibiting an agreed upon behavior.

TRUE

6. Time out is an effective method that is often done in the hall outside the classroom.

FALSE

7. Sociometric ratings are a direct measure of social skills.

FALSE

Short Answer/Essay

1. You have a group of 5 boys in the back of your room that do not want to stay on task in 9th grade Algebra. Whenever the material gets a little difficult, one of them will make a joke and get the whole group laughing. Though you do not want to keep telling them to be quiet, they really disrupt the flow of your lessons and make it hard for other students to learn. The lack of respect and disruptions are escalating the longer you ignore it. You were told that one of the boys has an emotional disturbance but you are not sure if he is causing the problem or not. How do you gain control of your math class without having to spend all your time on classroom management?

    a.   What are the strengths and needs of the students?
    b.   What additional information would be helpful to assess to make better decisions about these students?
    c.   What are 3 possible modifications or interventions you could use to help these students be successful and behave well in your math class?

    a.   Strengths: Friendships and a sense of humor. Needs: To not get you off-task, lack of respect, disruptions
    b.   Who is the ringleader? Which student has the problem? What are their academic levels? Is this a student who is frustrated so he would rather be disruptive than face algebra? Or is this a student who needs a lot of peer attention?
    c.   Possible answers: 1. Split up the gang of five. Get to know them as individuals. See if the problem goes away or only involves one or two of them. 2. Keep them after class and let them know the behavior cannot continue. You can offer them solutions or brainstorm with them. Possibly implement behavioral contracts with them, individually. 3. Call their parents or guardians and make a big deal of it. Try and enlist parental support. Most of all do not ignore it any longer or it will continue to get worse.

2. Give an example for each of the following recording techniques: Examples will vary.
- Event recording (recording each time a behavior occurs)
- Duration recording (recording how long a behavior occurs)
- Interval recording (recording length of behavior over small blocks of time)
- Time Sampling (recording at a set time if the behavior is happening or not)

3. When will proximity lessen or stop misbehavior in your classroom? What would you do if the misbehavior did not stop when you walked nearby?

If the student is doing a behavior that they do not want you to see, and they are aware of your presence, then proximity will usually stop it since they realize you will "catch them". But if the student is unaware of you, you may need to tap his or her desk, or signal to the student as you walk by. If the student is aware of you and continues to defy you, you may need to ask them quietly to stop or use whatever management system you have in place (take away a point for example).

4. If you find a child with no friends in your classroom is there anything you can do? Should you get involved? Why or why not?

The answers will vary but the point is to recognize that this may be a mild or serious problem that needs addressing. You should get involved and there are things you can do. You will need to assess the situation first. If the student needs some social skills you may have to assist with them. If the student is shy you may need to put them in safe situations with others. Peer tutoring may assist the student to get to know other students in the class. Student isolation is a situation worth monitoring.

Chapter 8: Promoting Inclusion with Classroom Peers Answer Key

Multiple Choice

1. Upper elementary students trained to interact with students with severe disabilities is an example of which program?

    b. Special Friends

2. An important first consideration in preparing a peer assistance program is to

    a. determine the precise nature of the situation that requires assistance.

3. Which is a step toward employing an effective peer tutoring program?

    d. All of the above

4. Peer social initiation is used for

    d. promoting social interaction with withdrawn children.

5. The most consistent benefits of peer tutoring are realized by

    b. tutees.

6. Which is true of cross-age tutoring?

    b. Tutors may keep a tutoring notebook

7. How often are 35-minute classwide peer tutoring sessions recommended to be used?

    c. Three times per week

8. In Peabody classwide peer tutoring, "Paragraph Shrinking," students

    b. say the main idea in 10 words or less.

9. Which are appropriate considerations when planning cooperative groups?

    d. All of the above are important considerations

10. Which is NOT a recommended cooperative group activity?

    b. Students compete in groups to be group leader.

True or False

1. One important use of peer assistance is in assisting students during emergency situations.

TRUE

2. In cross-age tutoring, roles of tutor and tutee alternate.

FALSE

3. Collaborative skills need not be taught as precisely as academic skills.

FALSE

4. Peer mediation strategies can be used to manage conflict situations among peers.

TRUE

5. Individual accountability is not necessary with cooperative learning.

FALSE

6. Jigsaw is a cooperative learning method for putting together puzzles.

FALSE

7. Peer tutoring is mainly used for increased socialization rather than instructional purposes.

FALSE

Short Answer/Essay

1. Janice is a sweet girl in your seventh-grade science class. She has mild mental retardation and has some awkward motor skills. She reads several years below her peers and she writes very slowly. She walks with a mild limp too. Janice is nice to others and tries very hard to follow your directions. In your science class you usually lecture then divide the class into cooperative groups for hands-on experiments. She usually can do the hands-on parts but is not able to write the lab reports. Janice is so slow at copying down the steps to the experiment that she rarely has time to complete the hands-on part in class. Due to her delays, no one wants to be in her cooperative group.

      a.   What are the strengths and needs of the student?
      b.   What are 3 possible modifications or interventions you could use to help Janice to be successful with her science lab?

    a.   Strengths: Nice personality, works hard. Needs: Assistance from peers for science labs.
    b.   Possible answers: 1) Instead of having Janice copy the notes, give them to her. 2) Let Janice be the first one to start the experiment. 3) Janice's group will benefit from her being in the group since she will have gotten them started (possibly with a little of your assistance) while everyone else is copying the board. This should give a little incentive to members of Janice's group.

2. Some research on cross-age tutoring matches older students with disabilities with younger students who do not have disabilities. Do you believe this would work? What do you see as possible pros and cons?

Answers will vary. There is some research saying that this method has been successful when pairs were matched carefully.

3. Under what circumstances would cooperative learning and peer-tutoring not be beneficial methodologies for your classroom?

Answers will vary but are located under Potential Limitations section of the text. Some other concerns with peer tutoring and cooperative learning is that they will not be successful if the students do not have the prerequisite skills or knowledge to work on the task together. These methods also do not work well if there is poor classroom management.

4. The roles for some cooperative learning groups are as follows: reader, recorder, getter, starter. Which roles may inappropriate for the following students?
- A student with significant reading delays (reader or recorder)
- A student with difficulty writing (recorder)
- A student with visual impairments (reader)
- A student who likes to throw materials around (getter)

Chapter 9: Enhancing Motivation and Affect Answer Key

Multiple Choice

1. Which is NOT a precondition to increasing motivation and affect?

    b. Create an environment where students compete for rewards

2. Students are more motivated to learn when teachers:

    b. Use positive feedback

3. In _____ students are evaluated with respect to previous performance and not against the performance of others

    a. task-oriented classrooms

4. Goals should be:

    c. Realistic and attainable

5. Marcy believes the reason she failed history is because the teacher doesn't like her. This is an example of

    d. negative attributions.

6. Which of the following statements is NOT true:

    b. Enthusiasm is frequently over-used.

7. One of the effective uses of praise is that praise:

    b. Should indicate the relation between effort and achievement.

8. Cognitive conflict refers to

    d. situations that are not easily predictable or explainable at first.

9. Overjustification occurs when

    b. interest is high and rewards are very tangible.

10. According to Richards La Voie, fairness means

    c. everyone is treated according to individual needs.

True or False

1. Intrinsic motivation refers to the participation in an activity in anticipation of an external reward.

FALSE

2. Common external rewards for school children are pencils, stickers and treats.

TRUE

3. Students with special needs are generally more motivated to achieve in ego-oriented classrooms.

FALSE

4. "I passed the test because I got lucky" is an example of a negative attribution.

TRUE

5. "I failed the test because I did not study" is an example of a negative attribution.

FALSE

6. Teacher enthusiasm variables include use of a varied choice of words.

TRUE

7. Regardless of disability area, all students with special needs enjoy novelty in their environments.

FALSE

Short Answer/Essay

1. You have been told that Julian is a gifted student, so you were excited to get him in your 8th grade English class. Unfortunately, he spends most of the time making snide comments under his breath to the other students to get a laugh at your expense. When you confront him, he does stop, but then draws pictures, reads novels, or engages in an off-task activity. When you ask him to show you his work he says he will do it later. His work is passable when he gets around to doing it, but you think he is bored and completely unmotivated. You can't raise the level of teaching in your class since the majority of your students are having trouble keeping up with the pace you set. How do you teach your class, but also meet Julian's needs?

    a. What are the strengths and needs of the student?
    b. What are 3 possible modifications or interventions you could use to help Julian to learn in your class?

  a. Strengths: Intelligent, has interests. Needs: Bored, Off task, Unmotivated.
  b. Possible answers: 1) Find out what Julian is interested in. What are the novels he is reading? You may be able to plan an independent enrichment activity around his interests. 2) Would he be interested in attending a 9th grade class? See if there are opportunities of acceleration at your school. 3) Get him reading and writing for a purpose. Is there a school newspaper or yearbook that he could get involved with?

2. What are two examples of educational games you can play in your classroom to motivate your students?

Answers will vary. Most teachers are familiar with Math or Spelling Bingo, Hangman, or other teacher made games where the students have to answer questions to progress on a board game.

3. Students are motivated when given appropriate levels of work. What does that mean? How do students behave when the work it too easy? How do students behave when the work it too difficult?

Answers will vary. Work that is challenging but not too easy is usually at a level where we can do 80–90% correctly. More than that we get frustrated, but always getting it 100% correct is boring. Students will misbehave in a variety of ways when they are not given appropriate levels of work.

4. Praise is effective if it is specific to the situation. It is also better when it is sincere. Which of the following are effective examples of praise? Can you rewrite the ineffective examples to be more effective?

- I like the colors you are using in that painting. (Effective)
- Wow, you are a great athlete! (Too vague)
- You look pretty today. (Too vague)
- That is a nice outfit you are wearing. (Effective)
- When you had all of the visual aids with your book report, it really made it interesting. (Effective)
- You did nice work on the test. (Too vague)
- Your story was very well written and it kept my interest until the end. I could not wait to see what happened next! (Effective)
- You are going to be the next Einstein! (May be an exaggeration- less sincere)

Chapter 10: Improving Attention and Memory Answer Key

Multiple Choice

1. Students in which disability category may exhibit difficulties sustaining attention?

    d. All of the above

2. _____ is memory of facts and concepts about the world, known independently of one's personal experiences.

    a. Semantic memory

3. _____ is a term that defines the metacognitive process of knowing about memory.

    b. Metamemory

4. Creating a mental picture to assist in memory is an example of

    b. imagery.

5. An example of an enactment is:

    c. Doing a relevant activity, rather than reading or hearing about the same information

6. The keyword method can be used effectively for remembering:

    d. All of the above

7. _____ are rhyming words for numbers, and are useful in learning numbered or ordered information.

    a. Pegword strategies

8. The HOMES strategy to prompt recall of the names of the Great Lakes is an example of

    d. letter strategy.

9. A good pegword for seven is:

    b. Heaven

10. Using the phrase "My Dear Aunt Sally" to remember procedures in mathematics is an example of a(n)

    a. acrostic.

True or False

1. Directly asking students to pay attention can improve their attention.

TRUE

2. Self-recording systems for attending often employ a timer.

TRUE

3. Self-monitoring of attention is usually more effective than self-monitoring of performance.

FALSE

4. Clustering refers to grouping different types of information by category, and then rehearsing the information.

TRUE

5. A good keyword for "celebrate" could be "party."

FALSE

6. Pegwords are rhyming words used to represent numbers, such as "hive" for five.

TRUE

7. Visual aides can assist a student's memory of a concept.

TRUE

Short Answer/Essay

1. Jezebel is a student in your second-grade class with moderate mental retardation. She is not able to read words, but she does know how to identify letters and her numbers most of the time. You are working with the special education teacher on an alternative curriculum for her. One of the IEP objectives states that she will be able to count up to 9 items and then point to the corresponding number. You are having her count

pictures on a worksheet then circle the correct number. Jezebel can only do it with assistance. What else can you try to help improve her memory?

    a.   What are the strengths and needs of the student?
    b.   What are 3 possible modifications or interventions you could use to help Jezebel to be successful on the IEP objective?

    a.   Strengths: Knows numbers and letters by sight. Needs: To understand counting and numbers concepts.
    b.   Possible answers: 1. Use manipulative for counting. Jezebel needs to understand the concepts concretely first. 2. Do a task analysis. Possibly have Jezebel just learn to count to 3 at first. 3. Make the task into a game. Since Jezebel needs a lot of repetition she needs to be motivated. Computer drill and practice program may help once she can do some counting with objects.

2. How do you get information from short-term memory to long-term memory? Give examples of how you remember a new phone number that you do not want to have to look up.

The way information is stored in long term memory is through rehearsal. But strategies and mnemonics will help. Some people have to use their fingers to remember phone numbers. Other people have elaborate strategies such as remembering ball players with the same numbers on their jerseys as in the phone number.

3. What is a mnemonic you have used in the past? Can you make one up on the spot? For example, how do you remember which is the symbol for greater than (>) or less than (<)? Most people use a mnemonic device. Can you devise a mnemonic for how to spell the state that you live in?

Examples will vary. The most common mnemonic for greater than is that it is the mouth of an animal or character (i. e.: Pacman, a shark or an alligator); after drawing the picture all you need to remember is they always want to eat more! The state examples are usually even more creative.

4. What factors impact memory? If you are tired, how good is your memory? What happens to a student's memory if they are upset, or hungry, or distracted by a classmate?

Answers will vary. The point is to be sensitive to the other variables affecting attention and memory.

Chapter 11: Teaching Study Skills Answer Key

Multiple Choice

1. A good way to help students keep track of long-term and short-term assignments is:

    b. Demonstrate how to use daily planners

2. The process of taking a large task or assignment and breaking it into smaller tasks is known as

    c. task analysis.

3. When assigning homework, it is helpful to:

    d. All of the above

4. Homework should not be assigned unless:

    b. Students possess skills and knowledge to complete it independently

5. The LINKS strategy is intended to help students with

    b. note taking.

6. The 'W' in the AWARE strategy stands for:

    b. Write quickly.

7. The difference between the three-R and five-R strategies is that the five-R strategy includes

    c. more after-lecture studying steps.

8. If a note taker is too slow, one appropriate strategy is:

    b. Provide a basic outline as a handout

9. To help students decide what to write in notetaking:

    d. All of the above

10. INSPECT is a proofreading strategy to be used with

    a. word processors.

True or False

1. Many students with disabilities lack effective study and learning strategies.

TRUE

2. Task analysis is a strategy for determining how important a task is.

FALSE

3. Self-monitoring sheets can be helpful in meeting class work expectations.

TRUE

4. The first important listening skill is "determine the purpose."

TRUE

5. One way to improve your students' listening skills is to adjust your lecture to include key words or cues.

TRUE

6. "Partial outline" means that students complete outlines for only the first part of the teacher presentation.

FALSE

7. There is no best way to make a study outline for students with special needs.

TRUE

Short Answer/Essay

1. You teach a high school history class. John has average intelligence but also has a hearing impairment that prevents him from taking good notes in your class. He reads from the book well, but you like to test students from the discussions and lectures as well. He has a hearing aid and he sits in the front row. But he still misses a lot of what you say since you walk around the room when lecturing.

      a.   What are the strengths and needs of the student?
      b.   What are 3 possible modifications or interventions you could use to help John to be successful taking notes?

  a.   Strengths: Average intelligence, good reading skills, sits up front. Needs: Missing lecture notes.
  b.   Possible answers: 1. John can get the notes from another student by either copying them or having the student use carbon paper. 2. You can give John a copy of your lecture notes so you know he has the information. 3. John can use an amplification device such as an auditory trainer to hear you lecture.

2. Why might you need to teach students how to use a table of contents or a glossary? How will these skills help all of your students, especially students with learning disabilities?

Students need to learn reference skills in order to learn from reference materials. Rather than randomly flipping through pages to find information, knowing how to use a table of contents or how to look up a word in the glossary can help the efficiency of your students' research time. Students with learning disabilities often have problems with organization and reference skills will assist them to organize their search for information.

3. There is research evidence that individuals who learn test-taking strategies do better on tests. What test-taking strategies do you use for tests? Which of these would be helpful for your students to learn, especially your students with test-taking problems?

Examples will vary. Teachers should be aware of their own learning strategies (meta cognition). There are several examples in the textbook of how students can learn including the use of specific study skills strategies that have been researched. There is more information on this topic in the next chapter.

4. Write a task analysis for looking up a word in a dictionary. How many steps does it take? What prerequisite skills do you assume the student has already?

Task analysis step will vary.

Chapter 12: Assessment Answer Key

Multiple Choice

1. Which assessment is a collection of students' products and other relevant information collected over time?

      c. Portfolio assessment

2. Which is a testing modification for norm-referenced tests?

      d. All of the above

3. "Matching" test formats can be made easier for students with special needs to use by:

    b. Matching the number of items in each column

4. Curriculum-based measurement can be very effective in improving the achievement of

    d. all students in inclusive classrooms.

5. Performance assessment is particularly useful for students with disabilities because:

    c. Students can demonstrate what they know on "real" tasks

6. General preparation strategies for tests include which of the following:

    d. All of the above

7. Elimination strategies involve removing

    b. answer choices known not to be correct.

8. Which is an effective strategy for math computation subtests?

    d. All of the above

9. Words such as "always" and "never," which should be considered carefully when taking a test, are referred to as

    c. specific determiners.

10. This strategy facilitates essay test performance.

    a. ANSWER

True or False

1. Curriculum-based assessment could include any procedure that evaluates student performance in relation to the school curriculum.

TRUE

2. Reliability and validity are not necessary for some types of tests.

FALSE

3. Deviations from standard administration procedures do not usually limit the usefulness of the test.

FALSE

4. It is ethical to modify tests for students with disabilities as long as you offer the same modifications to students without disabilities.

FALSE

5. Essay questions cannot easily be modified, since the student does most of the writing.

FALSE

6. One way of modifying grading for students with disabilities is to base the grading on goals and objectives in the IEP.

TRUE

7. The best way to modify grades for students with disabilities is to inflate them so they do not feel badly.

FALSE

Short Answer/Essay

1. Janie is a student who has cerebral palsy. She has average cognition but cannot write well or speak well. She likes to interact with others and has some friends in the class who seem to understand her. Janie is able to point but only if the object or area is larger than allowed by regular worksheets. She has a great attitude and works hard but you do not always know what she understands. Janie needs to take tests in several subjects this week. You hope she does well on them, but you need to make sure she can answer the questions.

    a.   What are the strengths and needs of the student?
    b.   What are 3 possible modifications or interventions you could use to help Janie be successful on her tests?

    a.   Strengths: Average cognition, some speaking and writing, friends, pointing, great attitude. Needs: Test taking formats that accommodate her disability.
    b.   Possible answers: 1. For multiple choice tests, Janie can point to a letter in a quadrant on her desk and you can record her answers. 2. If Janie has an essay test she can be tape-recorded. 3. For a math or spelling test Janie may need the format changed to multiple choice. 4. Janie may also be able to take tests if they are on computers and only need a mouse click.

2. What would be the best way to assess the following student skills or knowledge?
- Focusing a microscope (Performance Assessment)
- Basic multiplication facts (Curriculum Based or Criterion Referenced Assessments)
- Writing a paragraph (Curriculum Based)
- Eligibility for special education (Norm-Referenced combined with other assessments)

3. What activities can a teacher do to improve her students' with disabilities' performance on a norm-referenced test?

Use approved test modifications, use individually administered tests, teach test-taking skills, increase motivation, and improve examiner familiarity.

4. How would you modify the following test formats?
- Essay test for a student who is blind

Possible answers: Give the test orally, or on a tape recorder, or using a computer with text to speech.

- Spelling test for a student who has a significant hearing loss

Possible answers: Give him or her a written format with several options and he or she will need to choose the correctly spelled word, or correct an incorrectly spelled word.

Chapter 13: Literacy Answer Key

Multiple Choice

1. Snider (1997) states that some estimate that as many as _____ of students do not discover sound-symbol relationships on their own without explicit instruction.

      b. 25%

2. _____ has been defined as "the method of using sounds of a language when teaching people to read" (Fischer, 1993, p. 1).

      c. Phonics

3. Which statement is FALSE regarding an exemplary phonics program?

      b. Emphasizes memorizing rules, before reading words

4. _____ refers to the ability to examine structures of words and break them into pronounceable syllables.

      b. Structural analysis

5. _____ are irregular words that are used frequently at various grade levels.

      a. Sight words

6. Timing students' oral reading several days a week and charting their performance over extended time periods is an example of

      c. curriculum-based measurement.

7. Which of the following is a strategy to activate prior knowledge?

      a. TELLS fact or fiction

8. Which of the following is an example of a self-generated question?

      a. What are you studying the passage for?

9. The peer-questioning activity, "Sharing Chair," is intended to help students:

      b. Expand their ideas

10. The TREE strategy is intended to help students

      c. plan their essays.

True or False

1. A linguistic series teaches word families (cat, hat, sat, pat, mat) rather than individual letter sounds.

TRUE

2. Creating rhymes is an example of a phonemic awareness training activity.

TRUE

3. The SPACE strategy is intended to help students figure out unfamiliar words.

FALSE

4. Teaching prefixes, suffixes and Latin roots to students are all included in structural analysis.

TRUE

5. During reciprocal teaching, students assume the role of teacher.

TRUE

6. Repeated readings promote reading fluency in students with reading difficulties.

TRUE

7. Cover-Copy-Compare is a strategy for studying spelling words.

TRUE

Short Answer/Essay

1. Jerry is a student in your 4th grade general education class who has a learning disability. He is good at math but cannot read well. He thinks stories are dumb and would much rather play on the computer. He is not able to sound out written words he does not know or show interest in memorizing sight words. But he likes to tell stories to the other children about TV shows he watches such as DragonBall Z. He is somewhat disruptive during reading time since he is off task.

   a. What are the strengths and needs of the student?
   b. What are 3 possible modifications or interventions you could use to help Jerry to be successful with reading?

   a. Strengths: Tells stories, likes the computer, likes Dragonball Z. Needs to: learn reading, low motivation, has weaknesses in decoding and sight words.
   b. Possible answers: 1. Put him on a computer reading program such as Lexia. Try the phonics based one or the sight words based program to see which works better. 2. Have him tell you stories and you write them for him. Have him learn to read his own words (Language Experience Approach). 3. Get Dragonball Z comic books to start him reading.

2. Why is fluency important for reading? Adults usually are not asked to read aloud in most situations. Why are children asked to read aloud?

Good fluency usually correlates with improved comprehension. It is hard to comprehend what you are reading if you have to decode a lot of words. Good fluency is a great self-esteem builder. Many children want to sound good when they read aloud. We ask children to read aloud since we cannot hear them when they read silently! As teachers we want to know if they can decode the words as well as comprehend them.

3. Students with writing disabilities can now use word processing software on a computer. What are the benefits of using a word processing program on a computer? What are the problems of relying solely on computers for writing? What skills do students need to learn in order to use word processing programs?

Benefits: spell check, grammar check, easy to read, easy to edit. Problems: you do not always have a computer available and it takes a lot of prerequisite skills. Students still will need to know the alphabet, how to spell, and some keyboarding skills as well as word processing commands and computer skills. It is much more complicated than just picking up a pencil so computers are not a simple cure!

4. What are some ways to test students on spelling words they use in their writing? How can you encourage students to attempt words they do not spell well? What are 3 ways to improve your students' spelling?

Possible answers: Words from students' writing can be used for their spelling tests. If you only grade students on the total number of words they learn, rather than those attempted, they have incentive to attempt more words since it will give them more chances to spell correctly. You can improve their spelling by: using relevant words, providing relevant practice activities, distributing the practice times, using peer tutoring, and using mnemonic devices.

5. A new medical research study found evidence that students with dyslexia (reading disabilities) may have limited ability to hear sounds that rhyme. If their reading difficulties stem from an auditory perception problem, what would be some other ways to teach reading that do not require decoding? What methods would increase their skills with word attack and decoding?

Possible answer: Sight words, or whole language approaches. If they are not able to do phonics, then possibly try linguistic approaches (word families), or structural analysis, which are visual as well as auditory.

Chapter 14: Mathematics Answer Key

Multiple Choice

1. _____ is the concept that sets of different objects (beads, blocks, etc.) can be matched with respect to quantity.

      b. One-to-one correspondence

2. Students with difficulty writing numbers may benefit from the use of:

      c. Dashed-line numbers

3. In Touch Math, numbers higher than 5 are represented with

      b. double touch points.

4. Placing quotation marks around a quotient is an example of

      c. verbal elaboration.

5. Miller and Mercer (1993b) demonstrated a word problem solving sequence strategy that included which levels of instruction?

      d. All of the above

6. A strategy for helping students determine the priority of operations in an equation is

      c. My Dear Aunt Sally.

7. A bridge between multiplication concepts and facts is the use of

      a. count-bys.

8. The "ask for one, tell for one" strategy is intended to help students

      b. determine implied operations.

9. Which strategy or materials are intended to enhance the concept of equivalence in fractions?

      a. Fraction Burgers

10. Which is intended to enhance the understanding of negative numbers?

      c. Algebra tiles

True or False

1. Counting is important but is not a necessary prerequisite skill to addition or subtraction.

FALSE

2. "Count-ons" and "pattern nine facts" are strategies to assist students with division and multiplication facts.

FALSE

3. An advantage of modified long division is that it allows students to view the entire problem.

TRUE

4. Demonstration plus permanent model means that the teacher demonstrates the problem then the student models it back.

FALSE

5. Numbers in number lines can go in either direction, with higher number to the left or right. It depends on the preference of the student.

FALSE

6. That volume formulas represent the area of the base times a multiple of the height is an example of a "big idea."

TRUE

7. Self-monitoring sheets are known to be useful for students struggling with math problem solving.

TRUE

Short Answer/Essay

1. Jake has TBI and cannot use his arms or legs well. His speech is understandable but is very slow and laborious. Jake tires easily and cannot last the whole day at your middle school. So he takes your math class during second period. Jake gets around on a motorized wheelchair but has no educational assistance. Today

you are teaching algebraic equations and the students are writing answers on the board. How do you include Jake? How do you check his understanding?

 a. What are the strengths and needs of the student?
 b. What are 3 possible modifications or interventions you could use to help Jake to be successful with his math class work?

a. Strengths: can speak, and is mobile. Needs: to participate with board work without tiring.
b. Possible answers: 1. Put Jake is a group of 3 where each has an assigned role – reader, writer, checker. Jake can be the checker in his group. 2. Make the board work multiple choice so Jake can point or say just the letter. 3. Have Jake do a problem at his desk on paper when the other students are at the board, but if the others are in groups, he should be as well.

2. Is counting on one's fingers an acceptable practice for mathematics? What would be your rationale for encouraging or discouraging this practice among your students?

If using his fingers helps a student do better in math then he should go right ahead. There are several "finger tricks" to help students. The only time it should be discouraged is if the finger strategy is slowing down a student who may not need to use it anymore.

3. Teachers are encouraged to use manipulative materials to teach mathematic concepts. What would be appropriate manipulative materials to use with younger students that would be inexpensive? How about for older students?

Answers will vary. Younger students can use candy, buttons, or beans. Older students can use paper clips, pencils, or pennies.

4. The researchers say to teach word problems with concrete, semi-concrete and abstract concepts. Give an example of each for teaching a multiplication word problem to students in an elementary classroom.

Examples will vary. Concrete examples should use manipulative materials or real world simulations. Semi-concrete may include drawings or pictures, and abstract concepts can include multiplication problems or word problems.

Chapter 15: Science and Social Studies Answer Key

Multiple Choice

1. In a _____ approach, students undertake specific projects or experiments to enhance understanding of the subject.

 b. activities-oriented

2. Which of the following are examples of content enhancements?

 d. All of the above

3. The O in the acronym POSSE stands for

 b. Organizing predictions based upon the forthcoming text structure

4. Modified worksheets assist students with special needs by:

 b. Enabling students to keep up with the pace of instruction

5. IT FITS is a strategy to help students:

      c. Create mnemonic strategies

6. Which of the following is a distinct type of text structure?

      b. Cause-effect

7. After textbook reading activities, to promote mastery of content by all students:

      d. All of the above

8. Adaptations for activities involving magnetism and electricity include:

      c. Connect a light bulb to flash when constructing telegraphs

9. Adaptations for activities involving the "physics of sound" include:

      d. All of the above

10. Strategies for adapting inquiry-oriented approaches in science and social studies include:

      c. Use guided questioning

True or False

1. Students with disabilities and other special needs rarely encounter difficulties with science and social studies textbooks.

FALSE

2. Framed outlines refer to outlines students create within "frames" or units of content.

FALSE

3. Students familiarize themselves with the organization of the chapter during the "size up" pass in the MultiPass strategy.

FALSE

4. Though research supports the use of study guides, in science and social studies study guides will often confuse students with disabilities.

FALSE

5. One modification a teacher may make on a worksheet is to enlarge the font for a student with visual impairments.

TRUE

6. The TRAVEL strategy is designed to help students create their own cognitive organizers.

TRUE

7. In some cases, deductive thinking activities may be a positive alternative to inductive inquiry methods.

7. In some cases, deductive thinking activities may be a positive alternative to inductive inquiry methods.

TRUE

Short Answer/Essay

1. Jade is a visually impaired student in your fifth grade general education class. She is articulate and bright, but hates to be singled out more than necessary. Although she can see when things are enlarged and held close to her face (she wears very thick glasses), she could not see your demonstration during today's science lesson when you demonstrated how to make a cloud in a jar (you are teaching about precipitation). Tomorrow you want the students to duplicate the experiment and write up their findings.

     a. What are the strengths and needs of the student?
     b. What are 3 possible modifications or interventions you could use to help Jade be successful for her science experiment?

a. Strengths: Articulate and bright, some vision. Needs: Can't see experiment, hates to be singled out
b. Possible answers: 1. Jade can be your assistant and help with materials (so she can stand very close). 2. After you do the experiment and all of the other students are busy, Jade can come up for a closer look. 3. You carefully describe in detail everything you see so that Jade can follow along.

2. In many middle school and high school science classes, the students are assigned lab partners for science experiments. What characteristics would you look for in a student that you may pair up with a student with disabilities? Would you keep permanent lab partners or change them? How would a lab partner be able to assist a student with disabilities?

Various answers are acceptable. Sensitivity to the issue is what is being asked. If a lab partner pairing is not working well, there should be some modification. But even when a good lab partner is found, that does not mean a student with disabilities should not have to learn to get along with other partners. Lab partners without disabilities should also learn how to adjust to a person with disabilities.

3. A common modification for a student with lower reading skills is to give them materials from publishers that have science and social studies content, but written at a lowered reading level. Adolescents are very concerned about being perceived as different from their peers. How do you assign work to the student in this alternate book for homework without making it clear to everyone in the class?

There may be several solutions. One is that the student could have a folder with his or her assignment that is left in a prearranged location by the teacher. The student can get his or her assignment from the folder and turn in work. It is usually best to let the student use the same textbook in class (even if they can barely read it) and they can use their supplement at home. Being sensitive to an adolescent's feelings can really help in making inclusion work.

Chapter 16: Art, Music, Physical Education, Foreign Languages, Vocational Education, and Transitions Answer Key

Multiple Choice

1. Individuals with disabilities have exhibited outstanding achievement in:

     d. All of the above

2. Some adaptations for students with special needs in physical education do NOT include:

     a. Have students with disabilities play in another gym

3. Instructional methods used in foreign language classes rely upon good:

    d. All of the above

4. One helpful way to address safety considerations is

    a. developing a "safety profile."

5. _____ requires that vocational education for students with disabilities be delivered in the least-restrictive environment.

    b. The Perkins Act

6. Which of the following are modifications to the curriculum to initiate vocational and career education?

    d. All of the above

7. In vocational programs, goals and objectives should be

    a. realistic.

8. The three types of activities specified in individualizing instruction in vocational areas include:

    d. All of the above

9. The first step in the I PLAN strategy is to

    b. develop a self-inventory of strengths and needs.

10. After students with disabilities leave high school, they have rights under:

    a. Americans with Disabilities Act

True or False

1. Learning disabilities prevent individuals from high achievement in art, music, or athletics.

FALSE

2. Musical books and scores are cannot be printed in large print or Braille.

FALSE

3. Self-advocacy should only be taught to students with mild disabilities.

FALSE

4. Business education, marketing education, and health occupations education are all areas of vocational education.

TRUE

5. The purpose of a technical terms tabulation sheet is to document when a particular term will be discussed.

FALSE

6. Generalizable skills include a set of teaching strategies to promote generalization.

FALSE

7. There are several organizations that assist persons with disabilities with a variety of athletic activities.

TRUE

Short Answer/Essay

1. Jordan is now 14 years old and is getting ready for his first transition planning meeting. Jordan has spina bifida, uses a wheelchair, and has to use a shunt to control the build-up of cerebral-spinal fluid on his brain. He has mild hydrocepaphy, which caused some brain damage. He loves art and has shown some real talent with his cartoons. He says he wants to grow up to be an artist, but you are not sure if it is realistic since his academic skills are quite low. But you do not want to dash his dreams and tell him he should consider other plans until you know more about his options. What can you do to prepare him and yourself for this transition meeting?

    a. What are the strengths and needs of the student?
    b. What additional information would be helpful to have?
    c. How can you assist Jordan in reaching or changing his goals?

a. Strengths- loves art, has goals, Needs- low academic skills, wants to be an artist
b. Possible answers: Help Jordan to find out about art schools in the area and their entrance requirements. Help him to look up if there are other avenues for artists such as apprenticeships, or related jobs such as sign painting or freelance graphic arts. Jordan and you can look into local newspapers that may accept cartoon submissions. Check the Internet for options as well as examples of artists with disabilities.
c. Try to support his dreams as much as possible. He might get paid for his cartoons or artwork without going to art school.

2. If a student has significant delays in reading should she be excluded from art, physical education, and/or music so that she can have additional time for reading instruction or practice? Please give specific reasons for your answer.

Though answers will vary, a student should not be excluded from classes like art, music and physical education for basic skills like reading. Though reading is very important, a person with a significant reading problem is usually not "cured" with the extra time spent in reading and would be missing out on activities in which they may be more successful. Some additional time for reading may be beneficial, but not to the exclusion of all other activities. Can you imagine how you would feel or behave if there was one activity you were bad at, and you were made to do only that activity to the exclusion of activities you were better at?

3. An Individual Transition Plan (ITP) also concerns itself with the student learning daily living skills and having leisure interests. Is it the schools' responsibility to provide these skills or interests to their students? Why are these important? When are they provided to students that do not have disabilities?

Yes, one purpose of education is to assist in people becoming well-rounded citizens and successful adults. Daily living skills are important for anyone who will one day live independently. Leisure pursuits make life more enjoyable. Daily living skills are taught to students without disabilities in classes like home economics, health, and industrial arts. Leisure pursuits are taught in courses such as art, music, drama, and physical education.

4. Finding employment is a large undertaking for everyone. What are some of the skills all students, not just ones with disabilities, need in order to find and get a job?

Examples may vary. Some common answers are: job hunting, filling out an application, writing a resume, interviewing, and networking.